Contents

INTRODUCTION

MARKETING: WHAT IS IT?

**PACKAGING YOURSELF:
YOUR APPEARANCE/YOUR IMPRESSION**

PROMOTING YOURSELF: YOU CAN AND YOU MUST!

    How do I promote myself?
    The resume
    The cover letter
    The sales letter
    The application

MAKING CONTACT WITH THE HIRING MANAGER

    Personnel departments
    Help wanted ads
    Employment agencies
    "R&R" interviews
    Other job-finding strategies

GETTING THE JOB

    Interviewing for the job
    Negotiating the job offer

MAKING IT HAPPEN

    How to be realistic during your job search
    How to exercise faith during your job search

SUMMARY

BIBLIOGRAPHY

EXERCISES

SAMPLES

Intercristo's
CAREER KIT ™
A Christian's Guide to Career Building

•

Chapter Four
MARKETING:
"How do I get the job?"

•

By Dick Staub
and Jeff Trautman
•
Edited by Mark Cutshall
•
Illustrated by Martin Banke
•

Intercristo
Seattle, Washington

Unless otherwise noted, all Scripture
references are taken from
The Holy Bible, New International
Version, Copyright © 1978 by
New York International Bible Society.

Intercristo, Seattle 98133

© **1985 by Intercristo. All rights reserved**
Eleventh Edition published 1997
Printed in the United States of America

Library of Congress Cataloging in Publication Data

Intercristo

Career Kit: A Christian's Guide to Career Building

ISBN 0-933941-00-5

INTRODUCTION

Steve had sent out over 200 resumes and was still waiting for his first interview. Mary religiously read the help wanted ads in her local paper, but just couldn't find what she wanted.

John was working diligently on application number 47. He was "on file" with the personnel department of every company that hired for his line of work. His pencil was wearing thin and so was his patience.

Head hanging low, Sue stumbled through the front door of her apartment and threw the letter on the floor. Another thanks but no thanks rejection. Twenty-one interviews and not one job offer. Sue felt like she just couldn't win.

After one month in a job that didn't fit, Bill quit and decided to try another employment agency. Reluctantly he went downtown to a new firm, wondering if these people could find him the right job. Past experience kept his optimism in check, but the need for employment kept Bill hopeful. He waited his turn, and went to cubicle 8, resume in hand, hoping this person had an answer....

Getting the job. For a privileged few it seems to be no problem at all. However, for the rest of us, it's like looking for a needle in a haystack. Finding employment is one of the most difficult, taxing, confusing, and ego-threatening activities we encounter in life. Why is it so hard?

There are the obvious reasons like:
- The competition is just too tough
- I don't have the qualifications
- Nobody is hiring
- The industry is dying.

To a certain extent, these realities of the marketplace contribute to the difficulty of finding employment. However, there is a more widely shared reason why so many of us fail to find the right job. Simply stated the reason is:

We don't know what it takes to get the job.

That's right! The biggest barrier you face in finding employment is not knowing how to find employment. If you identified with Steve, Mary, John, Sue, or Bill, then this chapter will be of great help to you.

The goal of Career Kit is to equip you to take responsibility for making effective, Biblically-based career decisions. Getting God's perspective on work, assessing your design and desires, and exploring work possibilities are critical components that help you achieve this goal. However, as important and helpful as these first three chapters have been, there's more you need to know in order to achieve your ultimate goal of getting a job that's right for you. Until you learn what it takes to find work in today's marketplace, you could end up disillusioned, angry, and hopeless, and resigned to settling for less than God's best in your worklife.

The goal of Chapter Four is to equip you to carry out a thoughtful, reasonable, and successful search for employment.

The result is that you'll be able to secure work that fits you. Completing this chapter will build your career three ways:

1. Basic knowledge: You'll understand why job seekers with inferior qualifications but superior job-finding skills get work, while job seekers with superior qualifications but inferior job-finding skills remain unsuccessful in finding employment.

2. Sound Strategy: You'll learn how to make the time you invest in looking for work pay off. You won't have to wait around, feeling like you have no control over whether or not you get a better job.

3. Practical Skills: You'll develop the research and communication skills needed to identify job openings, get job interviews, and most important of all, get hired!

To benefit most from this chapter, decide now to base your job search on what we term "The 3 Rs" of successful job hunting: right thinking, requesting assistance, relevant action.

Right Thinking

How should you, as a Christian, be thinking about finding better employment? The following statements should shape your attitude.

"I'm not perfect, but I DO have strengths and experience that are needed and valued by an employer."

"God cares about my work and will walk with me in my job search. But this is no guarantee that the right job will be easy to find, or that the job search will not require disciplined, thoughtful effort on my part."

"I can exercise my faith during the job search by persevering in doing my part regardless of how I may feel from time to time."

To succeed in finding work, you must believe you have something to offer. You need to avoid equating God's care and guidance in your job search with how easy and convenient it is. And you need to learn how to make progress and take positive action in spite of your feelings.

Keeping your thoughts in perspective is critical to your success as a job seeker.

Requesting Assistance

When it comes to looking for work, no one goes at it alone. You can't get a job without the co-operation or consent of at least one other person—the employer who hires you. So, expect from the start that you'll need help to succeed in finding work, and that you should expect to look for and receive assistance throughout this process. Why? Because you have a valuable contribution to make and, therefore, you are worth helping.

Requesting assistance starts by making your job search a matter of prayer. Ask the Lord for guidance, wisdom, confidence, and hope each day as you faithfully pursue work that fits you.

Next, learn how to seek appropriate assistance in finding employment. We'll show you how this is done. Remember though, only you can choose to believe that you are worth helping, and then act on that belief.

Decide now that you will openly seek those individuals who might be part of God's guidance plan for your next job! Covenant now that you will not let anger, pride, or feelings of inferiority or stubbornness keep you from the insight, direction, and support that's yours just for the asking. Requesting assistance is a vital link in finding the right job.

Relevant Action!

Is it possible that you can diligently look for work and still not find it? Of course it is. The search for work is not just a matter of dedication and activity. Remember the old saying, "Dedicated incompetence is still incompetence?"

Unfortunately, most people who look for work spend a majority of time and energy in activity that yields minimal results. In this chapter, you'll learn productive job-finding skills and strategies. However, you must decide whether or not to implement them.

Choose now to learn, accept, and apply the information in this chapter. Become both a "hearer and doer" of the approaches that, when applied in faith, will yield tangible results.

As you move through this chapter and start looking for work, make these "3 Rs" the foundation of your job marketing efforts. Work at right thinking, requesting assistance, and relevant action.

The chances are good that, if you take these three steps, you'll find hope, encouragement, and ultimately the job that's right for you.

By exploring the marketplace, Jacob gained new vision for putting his unique strengths to work. With confidence and direction, he pursued work in many places, but finally he found his nitch at the Inn.

Like Jacob, you need a vision for putting your unique strengths to work. Now it's time to pursue work in many places as you seek to find your niche in the marketplace.

MARKETING:

What is It?

Chapter Four on finding employment is titled "Marketing: How Do I Get the Job?" because the search for work is essentially an exercise in marketing. Simply stated, marketing is "the process of identifying needs in the marketplace, and then filling them."

Marketing is a frequently-used but often misunderstood term. The chart below will help clarify what we mean by marketing, as well as demonstrate how marketing applies to your job search:

What is Marketing?

1.	Research the Marketplace Identify a Need	Substance To Clean Clothes
2.	Develop a Product To Fill the Need	Soap
3.	Establish a Price	$1.39
4.	Package the Product	Pretty Box
5.	Promote the Product	Ads—TV, Radio
6.	*Place* the Product in Front of the *Right Person*	Grocery Store/Consumer
7.	The Right Product, Meeting the Need, At the Right Price, Packaged and Promoted to the Right Person at the Right Place.	Closing the Sale

Explanation:

As you can see, an effective marketing plan begins with identifying a need. In this case, the need is for a substance to clean clothes. Once the need is established, a product is developed to fill that need. Ingeniously, someone came up with the ideal product: soap.

The next step is to put a price on the product. This is a very critical step. If the price is too low, the costs in producing the product won't be covered. However, if the price is too high, customers may not buy the product and once again expenses will not be met.

Once the product has been appropriately priced, it must then be packaged. A lot of money is spent packaging products so they'll appeal to the buyer. A pretty box is often the only distinguishing trait between competing products.

Once the product is priced and packaged, it must then be promoted. Promotion involves giving

7

the customer a reason to buy. Through radio, television, or magazine advertisements a company presents the product in such a way that the customer will see its value and want to buy it.

Once a customer is interested in buying the product, it must be easily accessible. Placing the product in a convenient, easy-to-find location is the next step in effective marketing. The more accessible the product, the greater the opportunity for a customer to buy. A great product can be overlooked if it is too hard to find.

Only when all these steps come together—the right product, at the right price, packaged and promoted to the right person, and placed in a convenient location—will the final step, a sale, take place.

This is what we mean by marketing. As indicated on the chart below, an effective job search follows this same seven-step process:

WHAT IS MARKETING?		**HOW DOES IT RELATE TO THE JOB SEARCH?**	
1. Research the Marketplace Identify a Need	Substance To Clean Clothes ➡	1. Research the Marketplace Identify an Available Job	Job
2. Develop a Product To Fill the Need	Soap ➡	2. Prepare Yourself to Fill the Need	You, the Candidate
3. Establish a Price	$1.39 ➡	3. Establish Salary Requirements	Salary
4. Package the Product	Pretty Box ➡	4. Package Yourself	Appearance
5. Promote the Product	Ads—TV Radio ➡	5. Promote Yourself	Phone–Write Resume–Interview
6. *Place* the Product in Front of the *Right Person*	Grocery Store/Consumer ➡	6. Make Personal Contact with the Hiring Manager	Hiring Manager
7. The Right Product, Meeting the Need, At the Right Price, Packaged and Promoted to the Right Person at the Right Place.	Closing the Sale ➡	7. The Right Person, Meeting the Company's Personnel Need, at the Right Price, Packaged and Promoted to the Right Person at the Right Place.	The Job Offer

First, you must identify a need in the marketplace. That is, an available job that fits you.

Step #2 involves preparation: getting the training and experience required for the job. Usually there are several different ways to achieve this goal.

Step #3 involves knowing your financial requirements and the range of compensation you will receive for this position. Just like a product, you need to know your price in the marketplace.

Step #4, packaging yourself, means realizing that your appearance is a significant factor in the job search. In the supermarket and in the workworld, visual appeal can be the difference in what a customer chooses to buy.

Step #5, promoting yourself, is a critical but often misunderstood part of the job search. As you will discover in this chapter, effective promotion makes a significant difference in getting a job.

Step #6, making contact with the hiring manager, is what getting a job is all about. If, in your job search, you are not talking with the people who make hiring decisions, you are not getting to the right people. Successful job seekers know how to contact the hiring manager before a job interview.

Step #7, the job offer, is an exercise in communication and relationship building. Those job seekers skilled in both areas turn job interviews into offers. Others who take interviews lightly, don't prepare, or abdicate responsibility for a good interview to the employer simply don't get jobs. You can become more successful getting job offers, if you're willing to work at it.

Getting the right job is a seven-step process. Each step is critical to your success in finding employment. At this point, you can probably identify where you can improve your marketing effort. Maybe you have not paid enough attention to your appearance. What about promotion? Have you avoided it because you saw it as bragging or not being humble? Have you been meeting with hiring managers during your job search? Or do you spend most of your time interacting with advertisements, applications, and agencies?

As we stated earlier, the biggest problem in finding employment is not knowing how to find employment. As you complete each step of the marketing process, you are eliminating this barrier once and for all.

A Quick Review

If you've completed Chapters One through Three of Career Kit, then you have probably completed the first three steps of the job search process. Let's review them in sequence.

Step #1: Targeting an Available Job That Fits:

Your work in the assessment and exploration chapters should have led you to an industry, field, and function that fits your design and desires. If you haven't clearly identified the kind of work that fits you, then go back to Chapters Two and/or Three, and complete them before continuing on.

Failure to target a specific job to pursue will make your job search more of a frustrating wild-goose chase and less of an exciting treasure hunt.

Step #2: Preparing Yourself to Fill the Need:

Although preparation has not been a major consideration in Career Kit, it is a reality each of us must face. If you aren't sufficiently trained or experienced to pursue work that fits you, then you must find a way to gain that training or experience. In Chapter Three you should have uncovered the various options available for gaining the qualifications you currently lack.

Whether you go back to school, take an internship, become an apprentice, volunteer, or start in a lesser position, you should have chosen a path of preparation before continuing on in the job search. If you are still unsure about the qualifications for the work you seek, return to Chapter Three and conduct several information interviews before continuing. There's no sense shooting for the stars if all you have is a slingshot.

Step #3: Establishing Salary Requirements:

WHO MAKES WHAT?

ONE WAY TO MEASURE THE PERFORMANCE, SKILL, AND EXPERIENCE NEEDED FOR A PARTICULAR JOB IS BY THE SALARY THAT POSITION DEMANDS. HERE'S A SAMPLE OF 1984 ANNUAL SALARIES:

JOHNNY CARSON	$5 MILLION
U.S. PRESIDENT	$200,000
AIRLINE PILOT	$ 87,000
THREE-STAR GENERAL	$ 66,000
FERRYBOAT CAPTAIN	$ 48,568
PERSONNEL DIRECTOR	$ 38,000
GARBAGE COLLECTOR	$ 33,384
CHEMIST	$ 33,000
NURSE	$ 25,000
BARBER	$ 20,000
PIANO TUNER	$ 14,000
CATHOLIC PRIEST	$ 6,000

THE SEATTLE TIMES

At this point in Career Kit, your financial requirements for work should be clear. In addition, you should have discovered through exploring the world of work what amount of compensation to expect for the job you're pursuing.

If you're still unclear on either of these points, then be sure you understand the whole financial picture before continuing on in this chapter. Pursuing work without a clear understanding of either your financial needs or earning power is like going on a blind date. By the time you see the whole picture, it's too late! Know your income requirements, and potential, in advance. Don't market yourself without these facts.

If you have successfully completed steps 1, 2 and 3 of the job search, then continue on in this chapter. The remainder of Chapter Four will be spent covering steps 4, 5, 6, and 7 of the job search. As stated in the chart, they are:

4. Packaging Yourself
5. Promoting Yourself
6. Making Contact with the Hiring Manager
7. Getting the Job.

STEP #4 PACKAGING YOURSELF:

Your Appearance/Your Impression

"Man looks on the outward appearance, but the Lord looks on the heart..."(I Samuel 16:7)

This verse was true in the days of Samuel, and it's true for you today as a job seeker. For better or worse, "Man looks on the outward appearance." Let's face it, we live in an image-oriented culture. Millions of dollars are spent every year giving products and people the "right look." From designer jeans to jogging shoes, commercials tell us to "look the part," "be in style," "play the role." Why? Because your appearance sends messages to those around you. It's like a storefront, billboard, or catalog picture; from your appearance, others form impressions about what's inside.

This is especially true when you encounter new situations, or new people. Remember Mom and Dad's response when you brought home your first date? Remember how closely they "checked him or her out?" Did they perceive this person as "All American," "counter-culture," "trendy," or "unfit" to be seen with you? Right or wrong, they formed first impressions. And these impressions either worked for your dating life—or against it.

Whenever you encounter others whom you don't know, and there is a lot at stake (be it a dating relationship or a job possibility), visual impressions become a significant source of information. They help to either confirm our expectations or feed our fears. Since how you look is important, be aware of the messages you send through your appearance. For example:

Your hairstyle can send messages about your personality. Are you trendy, conservative, traditional, etc.?

Style of dress may say something about your economic values —you're bargain basement or Fifth Avenue. And it can reflect your operating style—formal or informal, flashy or reserved, individualistic or conforming.

Grooming can send messages about your approach to work. Are you organized, detail-oriented, thorough? Or do you "look" unpredictable, disorganized, unprofessional?

Make a Good Impression

What messages will you be sending to potential customers (employers) about your product (you)? If you aren't sure what impressions your appearance is giving, here are some suggestions:

1. Ask several people in your chosen career field for suggestions and feedback about your dress and grooming. You can incorporate this step into the referral interviewing process discussed later.

2. Talk with someone you trust, who perhaps is more conscious of dress and appearance than you. Ask him/her for suggestions for how you can enhance your image.

3. Observe the appearance of others in similar positions where you seek to work. What style of dress seems appropriate?

When you go out looking for work, keep in mind that although you are a "used commodity," an employer wants to hire someone who looks as good as new. Isn't that how you shop for a used item: How appealing is a used appliance loaded with dents and scratches? Why do used car dealers dress up a car with new floor coverings, wax job, etc., before putting it up for sale? Most of us want a used item that looks like new. Before looking for work, make sure that:

- Hair is carefully groomed and cut. For women, hair should be shoulder length or shorter (especially for the business woman).
- Clothes should be recently pressed and cleaned.
- Shoes should be polished.
- Fingernails should be clean.
- All clothes should fit. Avoid baggy outfits or clothing that's too tight or too loose.

Another rule of thumb is to dress slightly better than you would expect to dress on the job. When in doubt, dress conservatively.

For white collar occupations, here are some suggestions for appropriate dress:

MEN	WOMEN
• Business suit (gray or navy) with white shirt with repeating pattern tie. Or:	• Skirted suit (navy or gray) with white blouse and pumps. Or:
• Sport coat (or blazer) and tie with matching pants.	• Belted dress, high-necked with minimal frills and a matching jacket.

Avoid strong colors for a shirt, blouse or tie. Also minimize jewelry, and avoid strong cologne or perfume.

For blue collar occupations we recommend:

MEN	WOMEN
• Sport shirt and/or sweater (tie optional) • Casual pants or slacks	• Sweater/blouse and • Pants/skirt

Once again, keep colors basic and matching. And leave your tennis shoes at home.

"Qualified" Applicants

Under no circumstances should you make contact with an employer unless you are appropriately dressed. Consider Jean, who, though well qualified for a job, showed up to drop off a resume in a sweat suit. (She had just been running.) The interviewer's first impression of her was less than stellar, and one that the employer never forgot. Consequently, Jean was never seriously considered for the job.

Then, there was Bob, a '60s radical who refused to shave or cut his hair. He complained about being unemployed, but refused to work on his grooming because "it's a free country." Bob's uncompromising attitude was reflected in his appearance. And it continues to be a stumbling block whenever he looks for work.

Moral: The worst time to begin an "accept-me-for-who-I-am" campaign is during a job search. Employers simply don't have the time to move beyond bad first impressions.

Last, there's Paul. He was a final candidate for a top-level position in a prestigious law firm. An unexpected rainstorm hit town just before the interview. Paul tried to avoid getting wet before the interview, so he wore an old parka to protect his suit from the unexpected spring shower. Once inside the building, he pitched the parka on a coat rack outside the employer's office. After a successful interview, Paul exited the office and picked up the parka. Unfortunately, one of the executives saw Paul walking out with his parka and communicated this to the person who had interviewed Paul.

Although Paul was a top candidate, the company could not risk the chance that Paul would wear a parka when he went to see a key account. He was dropped from any consideration. Paul saved a dry suit, but lost a job offer.

You may be sitting there thinking, "These stories are ridiculous. How shallow can people be! If that's the way they think, I wouldn't want to work there anyway!"

Be careful about this kind of attitude. Remember, everyone plays the "image game" to a certain extent. We all evaluate others on their outward appearance. Expect this in your job search, and prepare for it. Invest the time, energy, and—yes—money, in packaging yourself and leave a good first impression on your next potential employer.

STEP #5 PROMOTING YOURSELF:
You Can and You Must!

David was an outstanding free-lance illustrator. His work reflected the highest level of craftsmanship. There was a clear need for the quality of work David produced. Yet, he was living hand-to-mouth, barely making enough money to keep a roof over his head.

Why was this the case? Answer: Because David was uncomfortable promoting his services. He spent hours perfecting his talent to the exclusion of learning how to communicate this skill to others. David's low prices for high quality work reflected his own internal struggle to believe that his creative gifts had legitimate worth.

Through the help of a career counselor, David increased his confidence level and learned how to promote his services in a positive, appropriate way. Needless to say, business soared. Today, it's not unusual for David to have more requests for work than he can handle.

The difference in David's career success was learning how to promote himself to potential employers. Until he accepted the responsibility for promoting his own talent, and developed the skills to do it successfully, excellent work opportunities passed him by.

What about you? Have you taken responsibility for promoting your strengths and experience to potential employers? Or do you hold one of the following views towards promotion:

"If she can't see what I have to offer, it's her tough luck."

"I shouldn't have to sell myself—my experience speaks for itself."

"The thought of having to brag about myself to someone is repulsive. I feel so uncomfortable doing it."

These comments, and others like them, reflect a misunderstanding of the need and value of promotion in any job search. They reflect three common false assumptions about self-promotion.

1. It's the responsibility of the employer to identify your value.

2. Your value is obvious to everyone, and therefore requires no support, explanation, or interpretation.

3. Promoting yourself means you need to be plastic, phony, or insincere.

If these statements reflect your thinking about promotion, then consider the following realities:

Most employers lack the time, energy, and training needed to find out what you have to offer. If you want them to know, then you must tell them!

Unless you're in a small community where your abilities are widely known, or you're a highly publicized figure, then your value as a potential employee is hidden from view. Employers are not sages, they won't recognize your value unless you help them to see it!

WHO NEEDS ADVERTISING?
WHEN BUSINESS IS GOOD, IT PAYS TO ADVERTISE; WHEN BUSINESS IS BAD, YOU'VE GOT TO ADVERTISE.
ANONYMOUS

Think: How many sales, bargains, events, and/or opportunities have become a part of your experience because someone promoted them? How many times have you said, "I wish someone would have told me . . ." or, "Why didn't I get any information on that . . .?" Many opportunities come to us or pass us by, because of promotion. In our culture, promotion is not a cheap, superficial activity. It's a necessity.

Job seekers who can't or who won't promote themselves don't progress. It's as simple as that. So what does it mean to promote yourself? Basically promotion means: giving a potential customer a reason to buy your product/service.

As a job-seeker, you have a responsibility to give an employer a reason for deciding to hire you; employers aren't in the business of giving away jobs.

Is promotion a Biblical concept? Consider the following passage: "But in your hearts set apart Christ as Lord. Always be prepared to give an answer to everyone who asks you to give the reason for the hope that is in you" (I Peter 3:15).

Promotion is Biblical, and you can see it at work as you share your own faith.

You may never be a Billy Graham, but if you've committed your life to Jesus Christ then you ought to be able to sit down with one other person and share from your own experience why you're a Christian. After all, Christianity is not the only religion in the marketplace. In fact, the number of cults and sects seems to grow each year. Why should a non-Christian friend consider the Good News? From your own experience, what reason would you give him or her to seriously consider making a personal commitment to Christ?

Every Christian should be able to give a defense for the hope that is within him or her.

The same is true for you as a job seeker. You may never become a full-time salesperson. You may never promote another product in your life. However, you ought to be able to look an employer in the eye and give a defense for the hope (of being hired for a job) that is within you.

After all, you aren't the only person this employer will consider for the job. So why should he or she consider committing the job to you? Because employers need a reason to buy, you should have a defense, "a reason for buying,"

to give the person who is considering hiring you. That's what good promotion is all about; it's demonstrating your potential in a way that makes sense to the prospective buyer.

How Do I Promote Myself?

Effective promotion involves identifying and communicating three distinct dimensions of a product or service. These are features, benefits, advantages.

Let's take a closer look at each of these important dimensions of promotion.

Every product/service has features. Essentially, features are facts that describe the product/service. For example, if someone were to sell you a chair for your office, he or she might start out by describing the features of that chair:

"This is a fine chair, it's got a chrome-plated, three-pedestal base, swivel seat, padded arm rests, and water resistant polyvinyl covering!"

As you can see, describing the features helps the customer to think about what the product is like.

You are not a chair, but you have features that, once communicated, can help an employer better understand the product. Your features may be a college education, the ability to work with a particular firm/organization, former job experience, or past job titles/positions. Other features may include particular responsibilities you've carried out or knowledge about a specific product or operation.

Your features can also be character qualities such as flexibility, determination, diplomacy, decisiveness, or initiative. The point is you have distinct features that an employer would want to know. As you consider the particular job you'll be pursuing, what features about the product (you) would you communicate? In a moment you'll list the features that would be valuable to a potential employer. (If a music degree has no bearing on the job you're pursuing, then don't list it as a "relevant feature.")

In your first exercise, Marketing #1, you will identify the appropriate features you possess. These are the features you'll need to promote for the job you've chosen to pursue.

Turn to page 45 and complete Marketing #1 "Focusing on Your Features."

Welcome Back!

Features alone do not adequately promote a product. You must also consider a second element of promotion—benefits. What are benefits? Benefits are statements about the product that answer the customer's most important question, "What will this product do for me?"

Every product has distinctive benefits that need to be communicated to a potential buyer. Take the office chair mentioned above. You can see specific evidence for each of its benefits.

Benefits	Evidence
Reduces backstrain	"In a test group of over 300 office workers with back problems, 70% experienced less strain during their work day as a result of using this chair."
Maintains comfort and support after years of use and abuse.	"A ten-year survey of over 1000 users revealed that 80% were still using the chair. The report also indicated these users felt no substantial loss of comfort during that time period."
Molds to your unique body style	"Over here are two chairs used by two different clerks. You can see how both have been molded slightly differently, depending upon the body of each clerk."
Lasts and lasts	"Here are several letters written to us by customers who were amazed by the durability of this particular chair."

Note the difference between features and benefits. Features focus on the product; benefits focus on the potential buyer. You probably noticed that each benefit had supporting evidence. The reason for this is simple: If you're going to confidently tell someone what a product could do for them, then you want to have proof to back up your facts. Otherwise words are just dust in the wind.

You, too, have benefits an employer needs to know about. These are strengths that not everyone can bring to the job. Such strengths translate into benefits for the potential employer. The benefits you bring might include:
- Improved staff morale
- Increased production
- Increased revenue
- Satisfied customers
- Fewer errors
- Saving time and energy
- Reduction in expenses
- Consistent performance
- Expansion of program
- Meeting of deadlines
- Operating within budget
- Solution to problems
- More repeat business
- Faster service

An employer needs to see the benefits received from hiring you. This is where many people drop the ball in promoting themselves. In resumes and interviews, they wax eloquent about their features and neglect their benefits, when, as you've just seen, it's clearly the benefits that best promote a product.

To effectively promote yourself on paper, or in person, you need to clearly identify and communicate your benefits to a potential employer. In Marketing #2, you'll develop a list of specific benefits you can share in your next job interview.

Turn to page 46 and complete Marketing #2, "Building Your Benefits."

Welcome Back!

Hopefully, you've now targeted your top five strengths and benefits. You should add ten more to the list before you seriously start pursuing work. By developing a specific list of strengths and benefits you'll enhance your ability to promote yourself with accurate and concise communication. Now, let's move on to the third and final dimension of promotion—advantages.

Advantages are distinctions about one product that may not be present in another product. For example, a small car may get great gas mileage while a large car doesn't get good mileage but has lots of room. Depending on the buyer, one car has an advantage over the other. In the example of the chair, advantages might include:
- Lower price
- Lifetime warranty
- Ability to order factory direct and save money

- Only chair recommended by American Chiropractic Institute

To accurately promote a product, you must be aware of its advantages in relation to similar products.

You, too, have advantages over the competition. You have distinctions that will be appealing to the right buyer. When looking for work, it's easy to focus on your disadvantages. Or you may view yourself as too young, overqualified, inexperienced, too shy, too assertive.

Unfortunately, the more you focus on your disadvantages, the more convinced you'll be that you're not worth hiring. You'll take this poor attitude with you into interviews. You'll pass it on to employers and lose many employment opportunities.

How can you keep your disadvantages from becoming a barrier to getting a job? Though not easy to implement, the answer is simple: Discipline your thinking to focus on the advantages inherent in your disadvantages.

That's right! Start looking at the silver lining in the gray cloud. Focus on the possibilities rather than the problem.

Here are some examples to help you start turning your minuses into potential pluses.

"But I don't have as much experience as others who are also applying for the job."	"I am teachable, will not come in with my own biases, and can be employed for less money than a seasoned veteran."
"I've changed jobs so much in the last four years, why would anyone hire me?"	"When I see something I want, I know how to get it. Until now, the problem has been knowing what I wanted. The career planning I've just completed has given me a focus, and a reason for breaking the job hopping—starting with my next position."
"I'm too old. No one will consider me."	"I know my strengths, and have a proven track record. My experience will help me avoid a lot of mistakes, and my desire to keep learning will enhance my contribution."
"But I'm unemployed . . ."	"I'm immediately available to work at the right job."

Disadvantages and advantages. They are two different sides of the same coin, and you can focus on one side or the other. The choice is yours.

In Marketing #3, you'll develop a list of advantages to guide your thinking as you search for work.

Turn to page 48 and complete Marketing #3, "Affirming Your Advantages."

Welcome Back!

Knowing and communicating your features, benefits, and advantages is what promoting yourself is all about. It is your responsibility to give that potential employer a reason to buy. In completing this section on promotion, you've generated a list of features, benefits, and advantages related to your employment objective. This information will form the foundation for your on-going communication with potential employers.

The Resume

Your promotion effort is bound to take two forms during yor job search—verbal and written. Although the most effective form of promotion is one-to-one communication with the buyer (employer), you'll probably need to develop and distribute written communication that can be reviewed by prospective employers. In most instances, this means you'll put together a resume. So let's look at the "Five Ps" of effective resume preparation: perspective, purpose, principles, particulars, and problems involved in resume writing.

1. Perspective on Resumes

Getting a job is not a paper-to-people business, but a PEOPLE-to-PEOPLE business. Store this fact in your memory bank. The essence of finding work that fits is knowing how to make effective, appropriate contact with people.

Why state this now? Because

you need to realize that there's no magic in a resume. You can send out thousands of resumes and never receive an interview or job offer.

Repeat: Getting a job is not a paper-to-people business, it is a people-to-people business. Granted, you should have a resume, it does play a small but important role in the search for work. But the bottom line is that a good resume won't guarantee anything. In fact, a bad resume will even significantly hinder your job search efforts!

2. Purpose of a Resume

A resume is a written advertisement, and much like any advertisement it's designed to attract customers. In other words, a resume is one tool to help you get a job interview—nothing more, nothing less. The focus of a resume is to portray and promote your potential to any employer, to help him or her see how you could be of value. A good resume will accomplish this purpose.

3. Principles of Resume Writing

The marketplace is loaded with books on resume writing. It seems that everyone has a new approach to this precious piece of print. Rather than overwhelming you with all the alternatives and procedures out there, let's summarize the best effective wisdom reflected in many of these writings:

In general the shorter the resume the better. Advertisements are short, easy to read, and to the point. As an advertisement, your resume should follow suit. With few exceptions, keep your resume to one or two pages. An employer doesn't have the time to wade through pages on your personal background.

Focus your resume to a particular job. The one-size-fits-all resume is practically worthless. You should have a different resume for each specific position you seek. This means work, but it's worth it.

Writing a good resume takes time. No one writes an effective advertisement in one sitting. Most promotional literature goes through at least two or three drafts before it's finalized. Expect to rework your resume a few times in order to make it effective.

A good resume reflects accomplishment—and results. Most resume writers overwork their features and say little about their benefits. An effective resume is geared toward the employer's expectations and needs, not your past history. Your past is only significant as it relates to your future.

Avoid including any information on your resume that could initially work against you. These are referred to as "knockout" factors, and include age, marital status, religious affiliations, height, weight, personal photos, race, and any handicaps.

Don't include one or more of these items unless you're sure it will work to your advantage; otherwise, leave them out.

4. Particulars on Resumes

What makes a good resume? A successful advertisement projects an image of a product or service that:
- Grabs your attention
- Generates your interest
- Gives you enough accurate information needed to make you buy.

For your resume to advertise you properly, it must reflect these three characteristics as well. Here are some tips to writing an effective resume.

Make it eye-catching. Use a format that accents the part of your past that will appeal most to a potential employer. Basically, there are two formats —chronological, and functional:

Format:	Use When:	Avoid When:
Chronological	• Job history relates directly to position you are pursuing • Most recent employment is impressive or applicable • Job hunting in very traditional fields or industry	• Changing careers • Job history could reflect negatively on you • Been out of work a long time • Have no related work experience
Functional	• You want to emphasize strengths not used in recent job(s) • Changing careers • You've frequently changed jobs	• In traditional fields where previous employers are significant • Most recent employers have been prestigious

Samples of both formats are included on pages 65-73. The information should be appealing to the eye and easy to find. This is accomplished in several ways:

First, provide enough white space on paper so that the information does not look cluttered or wordy.

Second, use capital letters, bullets, underlines and/or typesetting to accent critical information.

Third, eliminate any abbreviations or words that are confusing, vague, or not widely accepted by the average reader.

Make it generate reader interest. There are four basic strategies to generate interest through a written advertisement. Each strategy has a specific application to your resume.

Strategy	Application
1. Target information to a specific need.	**1.** Have a written or unwritten job objective. Focus on the skills, achievements, and experience that specifically relate to that objective.
2. Include appealing facts and figures. Example: 10%, 3 days only! Everything must go!	**2.** Utilize facts and figures to accent your accomplishments. Example: Supervised 50 employees and increased revenue by 25%.
3. Use action words! Example: Come in today! Don't miss! Write now! Call immediately!	**3.** Note your accomplishments through action verbs. Example: Organized... Directed... Supported...
4. Include appealing testimonials. Example: Rated excellent by 97% of previous attendees! Excellent! (Movie critic, Sun Times)	**4.** Include an appealing testimonial. Example: "One of the hardest-working employees I've ever had..." Vice President of Accounting, Sunset System, Inc.

Be sure to photocopy your resume on quality paper. Contact a copy center or graphics firm to help you. We suggest using any ivory, off-white, beige, or gray colored paper. Avoid wild colors to attract attention, because that's all they really do. Whatever color of paper you use, get matching envelopes and additional stationery for cover letters.

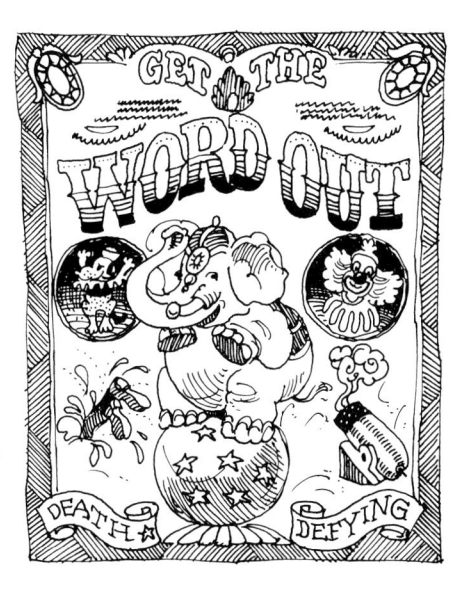

5. Problems in Resume Writing

Let's face it! Not everyone is a born resume writer. Some people don't feel comfortable with words; writing a one-page resume is like condensing the dictionary down to a greeting card. There is so much information you want to get across, it seems impossible to decide what to leave out.

Others struggle to believe they have features and benefits to communicate. Some people are perfectionists and are never satisfied with the finished product. Still others have a hard time getting an outline together.

If you struggle to put your resume together, then consider these few suggestions:

1. Find a few successful job seekers to help you write your resume, look at samples, and be open to learn.

2. Seek assistance from those friends whose gifts complement your strengths. They may have what you need (aptitudes for spelling or the ability to summarize information, conceptualize thoughts well, or outline and format data).

3. If possible, write and store your resume on a word processor. You'll be able to make revisions easily and quickly. Most cities have firms which offer this service for a reasonable fee.

4. Consult a career specialist in your area. However, beware of professionals who may want to charge you a fortune, or who've a set format for resumes. Remember, your resume should be unique because it reflects a unique person—you!

After all your hard work putting a resume together, take a few minutes and ask yourself these questions:

1. Is your job objective sufficiently supported in the resume? If not, what can you add?

2. Is there a logical flow to the information? Are your most appealing points stated first?

3. Does the information reflect action and accomplishment? Are your employment potential and benefits clearly communicated?

4. Is the resume easy to read? Are there short paragraphs, separated by white space? Or does it look like you'll have to wade through a solid, gray page of type?

5. Are similar words and responsibilities repeated? If so, how can you combine points and thus avoid redundancy?

6. Have you used the word "I"? If so, eliminate it. The entire resume is about you. There's no need then, to include "I" statements.

7. Have you used action words like organized, supervised, created, presented? If not, go through and insert these and similar verbs where they seem appropriate.

8. Is there any information that's irrelevant to the kind of work you seek? If so, eliminate it.

9. Avoid any negative comments. A resume should represent only your most positive abilities and traits.

10. Has someone else reviewed your resume for clarity, overall flow and grammar? If not, find a person whose judgment you respect for constructive critique.

RESUMES THAT SELL

THOMAS DEVLIN, DIRECTOR OF CORNELL UNIVERSITY'S CAREER CENTER, CAUTIONS THAT THERE'S A THIN LINE BETWEEN CREATIVE AND OBNOXIOUS (RESUMES). EXAMPLES OF SAFE APPROACHES MIGHT BE THE CORNELL GRADUATE WHO SNAGGED A REPORTING JOB BY WRITING A RESUME AS A MOCK FRONT PAGE OF A NEWSPAPER, OR THE WOMAN WHO LANDED A PROMOTIONAL JOB IN PUBLISHING BY BINDING HER RESUME IN A SMALL HARD-COVER BOOK.

EMPLOYMENT AGENCIES CITE AS FAILURES REAL ESTATE HOPEFULS WHO SUBMIT THEIR CREDENTIALS IN LEASE FORM AND PACKAGING-INDUSTRY APPLICANTS WHO SEND RESUMES WRAPPED AROUND AEROSOL CANS OR CEREAL BOXES.

THE WALL STREET JOURNAL

Cover Letters

In most cases, you should accompany your resume with a "cover letter." A cover letter helps personalize your communication and attract the employer's interest in your resume. An effective cover letter contains five basic points:

1. It's targeted to a specific person. No "to whom it may concern" titles/introductions.

2. It's written to appeal to the interests of the employer. Don't load your cover letter with "I wants." Rather fill it with employer needs, interests, and concerns.

3. Its first line should be an "attention grabber." (We suggest five such "grabbers" at right.)

4. The question "Why should I hire you?" should always be answered in the letter.

5. You should ask for an interview and take the initiative to follow up the cover letter to set an interview time.

As you can see, your cover letter is another promotional tool. Keep in mind you're giving an employer a reason to buy, so focus your letter on the employer, and his or her needs, expectations, and interests.

As mentioned earlier, a good cover letter will always have an "attention grabber" within the first few lines. Here are five basic ways to use a "grabber."

1. Reference a mutual acquaintance. Example: "Dick Strand, operations manager for Miller Industries, suggested it would be beneficial for the two of us to meet. Let me explain...."

2. Tell an "employment story." Example: "While teaching mathematics to underprivileged kids, I was able to raise student test scores by more than an average of 20%. The persistent and creative instructional methods used became a model for similar classes within the district...."

3. Ask a question. Example: "Can you use a mechanical engineer with the ability to maintain tight control over multifaceted problems, analyze complex problems and arrive quickly at some solutions? I have these talents, as demonstrated in the enclosed resume."

4. Give a compliment. Example: "I have used your products for years, and have been impressed recently with the new current line. Your 'Does It Easy' cleaner is everything you advertise it to be—and more.

"I am writing you because I want to put my knowledge in your products to greater use."

5. Promise a benefit. Example: "Throughout my ten years of sales training, I have consistently increased my students' sales volume by more than 30% within their first nine months of employment. Chances are I can bring this same level of success to your organization...."

Any of these approaches can be effective ways of inviting the employer (hiring manager) to take a closer look at the information in your resume.

For samples of effective cover letters, turn to pages 74-77.

What if I don't know the name of the person doing the hiring?

Then find out! Call the organization and say to the receptionist/secretary, "This is Bill Smith, and I'm forwarding some business information to the person in charge of central services. Could you give me his or her name and title so I can properly address my information?"

In most cases, using a direct approach like this will provide the person you need. Be sure to correctly spell the person's name. Also, make sure you have the correct job title.

Take the time to write a personalized, effective, business-like cover letter. Remember, this could be an employer's first look at you, so you'll want to make a good first impression. Be sure to keep copies of every cover letter you send. You need to know what you've said when it's time to follow up and pursue an interview.

The Sales Letter

Resumes and cover letters are not the only tools available for promoting yourself in writing. Another effective tool is called the sales (or broadcast) letter. The sales letter acts as a combination cover letter and limited resume. Its purpose is to expose employers to your potential, pique their interest, and cause them to contact you for further information. The sales letter is most effectively used when the jobseeker has a strong track-record she or he can promote. A good sales letter contains the following ingredients:

1. An attention getter—A past accomplishment in work that would be appealing to an employer.

Example: "As controller for a $14,000,000 agency, I automated the accounting department and cut expenses 20% in the first year."

Next

2. Explain your purpose in writing: "Your company may be in need of innovative but realistic leadership in the accounting department. If so, you might be interested in the following contribution I have made:"

Next

3. Further demonstrate your potential value to the employer: This is done by citing several previous work accomplishments that reflect your unique contribution. For example:

• Proposed to senior management a cost control department which was approved. Department was saving company money in two years.

• Completed over 25 extensive audits for a wide range of public and private business.

• As a member of a large accounting department (35 staff) decreased staff turnover by 15% through effective management practices. Also eliminated 500 hours of paid overtime through more efficient redistribution of work responsibilities.

Next

4. Develop your credibility. Cite experience, education, and training that would interest the employer.

Example: "As CPA with five years of 'big eight' audit experience and over ten years of diverse management responsibility, I would welcome the opportunity to discuss more fully the potential of working together with you."

5. Initiate contact with the employer: "I'll call you next week to pursue the possibility of working with your firm. Should you need to reach me sooner, my number is 754-8991."

Putting it all together, your sales letter might look like this:

Mr. William B. Barclay
Vice President for Finance
C.V.T. Corporation
Mainstreet, U.S.A. 97742

Dear Mr. Barclay:

As controller for a $14,000,000 agency, I automated the entire accounting function and cut operating expenses by 20% within one year.

Your company's accounting department may have need for innovative, realistic management. If so, you might be interested in the following contributions I have made:

• Proposed to senior management a cost control department that was approved. Department was saving the company money within two years.

• Completed 25 extensive audits for a wide range of public and private business.

• Managed a large accounting department (staff of 35), and decreased staff turnover by 15% through effective management practices. Also eliminated 500 hours of paid overtime through more efficient distribution of work responsibilities.

As a certified public accountant with five years of "big eight" auditing experience, and ten years of diverse accounting management responsibilities, I welcome the opportunity to discuss more fully the potential of our working together.

I'll call you next week to pursue the possibility of our working together. Should you need to reach me sooner, my number is 754-8991. Thanks for your time and consideration.

Sincerely,

Richard LeeMaster
1507 Mount St.
Somewhere, U.S.A. 73904.

The benefits of a sales letter are:
1. It's brief and to the point.
2. It can be widely distributed with minimal cost.
3. It can reflect your best contributions, so those who respond are looking for someone like you.
4. It gives you the opportunity to write a more personalized resume once the employer contacts you.

Keep in mind, the sales letter has limitations. First, although a personalized and targeted piece of promotion, it's still a direct-mail device. This means that to get results you'll have to cast your net very wide. You can expect that for every 100 letters you send out, only three to five employers will contact you for an interview. This is a realistic response rate.

Final Comments on Sales Letter:
1. Keep records of all your letters. For example, if you don't hear from an organization within three to four weeks, send a second, slightly revised letter. Always change your opening "attention grabber" or other parts of the letter. Take the time to keep your name and your employment potential before the employer's eyes.
2. Don't use this approach unless you have a relatively strong background to draw upon.
3. If you can make personal contact with the hiring manager, then do so. Don't send a letter just because it's easier. A one-to-one meeting is a far better way to communicate than a printed piece of paper.
4. Personalize each letter. Make sure each one is word processed individually, addressed to the right person, and personally signed by you.
5. Use high quality paper with matching envelopes. Remember, first impressions are lasting impressions, especially when you're looking for work.

Reviewing Promotion

Hopefully by now, you've gotten the message that self-promotion is a necessity. You are responsible for giving a potential employer a reason to consider hiring you.

Although getting a job is not a paper-to-people business, it does require some written communication. By following the suggestions in this section, the written materials you develop during the job search will enhance your chances of getting interviews—and rewarding work.

In this section, we'll address the most critical part of the entire marketing process—making contact with the hiring manager.

Before going any further, we suggest you stop here and revise (or develop) your resume. You can start by reviewing your most recent resume; critique it as a promotional piece. Ask yourself, "How clearly do I communicate my features, benefits, and advantages?"

Next, consider the value of your resume as a written advertisement. Does it grab the reader's attention? Does it generate interest? Is it easy to read? Is it accurate? Do you express achievement, include appealing facts and figures, and eliminate unessential information?

Don't continue until you have a finished resume.

SAKI'S MOUSETRAP

IN BAITING A MOUSETRAP WITH CHEESE, ALWAYS LEAVE ROOM FOR THE MOUSE!

SAKI

The Application

Resumes, cover letters, and sales letters can form an initial impression about you in the employer's mind. The same is true for employment applications. How you complete an application is important. Messy, hard to read, or partially completed applications can send negative messages to an employer.

Applications can also work against you. Information that's requested about salary requirements, marital status, and other personal matters sometimes may not be in your best interest to share.

What is the best way to complete a job application? Though there's no one right answer, here are a few suggestions:

1. Take time to type or neatly print every application. Never rush to fill out an application.
2. Make a copy of your first application and carry it with you to use as a reference for completing other applications.
3. When given an application, first scan it for information that may not be in your best interest to share. If you see such information, ask the person who gave you the form if there are any sections that don't require a response. Sometimes organizations use out-of-date forms and fail to communicate those items you can omit.
4. If you're asked to give an expected salary on the application, respond in one of the following ways:
- Write in, "salary negotiable."
- Write in, "unfamiliar with range for the position."
- Write in a range [Example: 21,000-24,000 year] slightly higher than what you expect to get. Don't write in a specific dollar amount or what you made on your last job. Most employers expect to pay you more than what you're currently making.

5. If you are expected to complete each part of the application, then do so! Leaving out information or writing "refer to resume" can be interpreted as laziness, or lack of cooperation. These aren't the traits you want to communicate to a potential employer.
6. Don't fill out an application unless you honestly want to be considered for the position. Nothing is more demoralizing in a job

search than completing an application for a job that half interests you.

By now, you should be well on the way to effectively promoting yourself through the printed word. To be totally successful, however, you must learn how to promote yourself verbally as well. And we'll highlight this important skill in the next step of the marketing process, "Making Contact with the Hiring Manager." Mastering this section may well make or break your effectiveness as a job seeker.

You may be saying to yourself, "Where is the Lord in the midst of all this promotional talk? All this talk about resumes, and image-building just sounds like the kind of suggestion I'd expect to read in any secular book on employment."

If this is what you're thinking, then our response to you is, "Yes, that's true." There's nothing inherently spiritual about the promotional section you've just completed. However, there's also nothing inherently spiritual about tuning an engine, completing a tax return, or repairing a tooth.

Each of these tasks requires a knowledge of what it takes to do the job. You won't get your car running, keep the IRS off your back, or fill the cavity in your mouth simply by praying and believing it'll all work out. There IS a spiritual side to these efforts. God CAN be glorified through a car repair, a tax return, or dental work. The point is, though, there's nothing UNspiritual about understanding and applying appropriate knowledge and procedures to a necessary and legitimate task like promotion.

In this chapter, we're showing you practical ways to apply your faith if you believe that God has a better place for you to invest your work. And, hopefully, you're gaining the practical promotional tools necessary to find the job you've now decided to pursue.

Regardless of how comfortable you are with the concept of "selling" yourself, we hope you'll see promotion as a legitimate skill that you can, and should, utilize in your job search. Remember, it's YOUR responsibility to give a potential employer a reason to buy. It's your responsibility to promote yourself.

STEP #6:

Making Contact with the Hiring Manager

The best product in the world is of little value unless the potential buyer knows about it. Think: Why do realtors hold open houses? Why do retail stores display their merchandise? Why do car dealers allow you to test drive an automobile? Why will mail order houses offer a 21-day free trial period for books and records? The reason is that a potential customer must be exposed to a product before he or she decides to buy. In other words, few individuals are willing to purchase a product sight-unseen.

A seller knows that only when enough potential buyers are exposed to a product that is properly promoted will sales take place.

Think of the parallel. The challenge for you, as a job seeker, is to find the best way to expose your product (you!) to potential buyers. The potential buyer is the hiring manager responsible for the department, or function, you've targeted for your job search. The manager is the one who makes the final decision about who gets hired. And it's this individual who needs to take a good look at you and your potential.

DON'T SIT IDLY BY

THE PEOPLE WHO GET ON IN THIS WORLD ARE THE PEOPLE WHO GET UP AND LOOK FOR THE CIRCUMSTANCES THEY WANT, AND, IF THEY CAN'T FIND THEM, MAKE THEM HAPPEN.

GEORGE BERNARD SHAW

Personnel Departments

Most people assume that the best way to get the necessary exposure is to visit personnel departments and fill out job applications. They're wrong. Ironic as it sounds, the truth is that a personnel department is more concerned with screening you out than helping you find employment. That explains why, in most cases, you'll receive very little helpful advice from personnel. Personnel officers rarely make hiring decisions. Instead they act as a screening device, weeding out potential employees according to some idealistic job description created by the hiring manager. This means that, although a hiring manager may be interested in you, personnel may screen you out on a technicality (example: you have only three years experience, and the job description calls for five). Do you see what happens when you entrust your job search to the personnel department? You introduce a middleman who makes decisions about you based upon an idealistic job description and his or her own perceptions and biases—which probably differ from those of the hiring manager.

The end result is very little exposure for you. No wonder visiting personnel departments can become discouraging.

IF THE TRUTH WERE KNOWN

FEW GOOD MEN COULD PASS PERSONNEL.

PAUL GOODMAN

Help Wanted Ads

What about responding to "help wanted" ads in the local paper or trade journal? Will sending in a cover letter and resume for a job opening give you the exposure you need? In most instances, the answer is "no." Why not, you may ask! Consider the realities of this marketing approach:

Reality #1. Most employers (approximately 80%) don't go public with their employment needs; over 80% of all available job openings never get advertised. Why? Because hiring managers are able to fill most of their needs through personal contacts and word-of-mouth referrals. Why announce their needs "out on the street" and be overwhelmed with applicants if you can find the right person within your own circle of contacts?

What does this "fact of life" tell you about help wanted ads? First, they are a poor representation of available job openings in your community. Second, they frequently contain openings that are hard to fill, jobs that most people either don't want (commission sales), or are not qualified for (chemical engineering).

Reality #2. Public advertisements invite such a large response that your resume or application receives very little attention. Your letter is literally one of hundreds. Unless you have superior qualifications or an "in" of some sort, chances are you won't even be considered.

Reality #3. "Help wanted" ads are not always indicators of an available position. "Blind job" advertisements (those with only a post office box listed) are often used by recruiting firms and employment agencies as a device to gather resumes. There may, in fact, be no job opening at all. Also, some organizations may be required by law or company policy to publicize openings, even if they have an idea of who'll be hired for the position. Consequently the interview process is nothing more than an exercise in conforming to the law.

Reality #4. Relying on the "help wanteds" does not get the product in front of the buyer; mailing your resume to an unfamiliar address simply puts a piece of paper in front of the buyer. Such an approach means limited exposure, and guarantees you only the slimmest possible chances of ever being hired.

Employment Agencies

Without going into detail, employment agencies also don't provide you with good exposure. The reason is that, like the personnel department, they too are middlemen in the job market. Sure, the agency has exposure to many potential employers. But you only get exposure to a few buyers—ones they decide to tell you about.

The biases and financial needs of the employment counselors often take precedence over your own employment needs. This isn't to say don't go to an agency. Rather, an agency isn't the only way nor is it the best way to get the exposure you need.

What IS the best way to give you (the product) the sufficient exposure to potential buyers (hiring managers), so that a sale (job offer) will occur?

"R & R" Interviews

The most successful strategy we at Intercristo know for getting the exposure needed for finding work is called the "R&R" interview. The two Rs stand for "Be Remembered" and "Be Referred." The genius of this approach is that it gives a potential employer sufficient exposure to you so you'll be remembered for immediate or future openings. In addition, you may also be referred to other hiring managers who may have an interest in meeting with you.

In an R&R interview you simply schedule brief appointments with a potential hiring manager. Your objective is not to ask him or her for a job but to talk about your interests and strengths, and to solicit any advice or suggestions he or she may have for your job search.

Here's an example of how an R&R interview works:

Jim was a counselor looking for a specialized position. He was encouraged by a friend to talk with Bill, the executive director of an organization involved in similar work. Jim and Bill met on two occasions. They discussed Jim's job objective in light of the organization's current needs and future direction. Although Bill was interested in Jim's ideas, he had no position, let alone openings, in his organization.

Jim continued to look for work and was eventually hired in a non-counseling job. One year later, Bill thought the timing was right for his company to develop a job similar to the one he had discussed earlier with Jim. Remembering their positive conversations, Bill contacted Jim and the two met for lunch.

Over a period of weeks, both men began discussing and outlining the details for this type of job. Ultimately, the position was created and Jim came on board.

A Cinderella story? Not really. Taking the initiative to contact hiring managers can in fact lead to job possibilities. It doesn't mean you have to wait a year, either.

WHICH ARE YOU?

THERE ARE THREE KINDS OF PEOPLE IN THE WORLD: THOSE WHO MAKE THINGS HAPPEN, THOSE WHO WATCH THINGS HAPPEN, AND THOSE WHO WONDER WHAT HAPPENED.

ANONYMOUS

Consider the story of Allison, a 19-year-old, looking for her first full-time position. Allison had decided to go into banking, and she thought the best way to enter the industry was to start as a teller. Allison contacted the personnel office at a big bank to inquire about positions. She was told they weren't accepting any applications.

Determined, Allison tried a different approach. She started contacting the branch managers of several large banks in her neighborhood. Briefly, she explained her interest in banking and asked for an appointment to talk personally with the managers. One executive was impressed with her assertiveness. And, having an opening for a teller-trainee, the executive decided to offer Allison the position. Within a matter of weeks, she was working full-time as a teller.

Jim's and Allison's stories can be yours as well. Learn how to set up and conduct R&R interviews, and open new doors to the job market. The greater the number of hiring managers who become exposed to your background and potential, the greater will be your chances of landing a job that fits you. In fact there are seven specific advantages of using the R&R interview as a marketing tool:

1. You, the product, get direct exposure to the potential buyer. In a one-on-one appointment you provide the hiring manager with an "open house" opportunity, a free look at a potential product.

2. By not asking for a job directly, you take the pressure off the employer of having to say "no" to you. You don't hide the fact that you're looking for work. After all, a job is your primary goal. But by communicating that you don't expect a job offer, the hiring manager is put more at ease to communicate with you.

3. By contacting hiring managers who have no apparent job openings, you begin tapping into the network of contacts most employers use to fill positions. Thus, this approach can help you uncover previously unknown job possibilities.

4. You gain solid advice, counsel, and direction from individuals who have the knowledge and perspective you need. This might include tips on job leads, the names of other managers to contact, and suggestions for improving things like your resume or appearance.

5. You take an active, responsible role in finding employment. No more waiting around for someone to phone you and feeling like there is nothing you can do to help your cause. The R&R approach enables you to exercise your faith through relevant action.

6. The hiring manager gets the opportunity to play the role of "expert" by offering you advice. This is a role that few people (hiring managers included) are asked to play.

7. You wind up receiving much greater exposure than if you were one of a hundred applicants. If your time with this person is mutually rewarding, then you'll have an edge on the competition for future job openings. This type of exposure is the best way to get job interviews.

There are other benefits to interviewing a hiring manager, but these seven should convince you of one thing: that using this approach for marketing yourself is effective because it's mutually beneficial to both you and the hiring manager.

You may be saying to yourself, "It sounds great, but I could never make this kind of contact. I wouldn't know where to start, or what to say." For most people, this response is a natural. You may not be used to taking such an assertive approach to finding work. Also, you may not be familiar with the methods needed to successfully implement the R&R approach.

Last but not least, even when you see the value and know the methods, you may still find this a difficult approach to use.

Considering all of these barriers, however, most people are able to succeed in finding employment by using this most effective job search strategy.

Getting a job is a people-to-people business. It requires knowing how to make contacts and build relationships with those individuals who can help you reach your job objective. In this next section you'll learn how to exercise your faith in the job search by diplomatically and deliberately initiating contact with potential employers.

Setting up "R&R" Interviews

Effective R&R interviews involve four steps:

Step #1: Targeting Potential Hiring Managers

The first and most obvious question to ask when using the R&R approach is, "How do I locate potential hiring managers to contact?" One answer is to start with the people you know.

"But no one I know is a hiring manager for the position I'm looking for," you say.

That's fine, your contacts can still be helpful to you. Remember in Chapter Three we introduced the concept of networking (access information by talking with those who might have the information you lack). Through networking, you're rarely more than four contacts away from anyone in the world. In other words, it's not unlikely that someone could locate a minister in Venice, Italy, by making four separate phone calls.

If you're already casting a skeptical eye at this idea, then we challenge you to give it a try. The fact of the matter is you know people who can lead you to hiring managers. By "networking" with these individuals, you'll be assured of gaining access to the managers who can help you.

DO THE IRISH KNOW?
LUCK IS THE RESIDUE OF DESIGN.
BRANCH RICKEY

So where do you start? Generally speaking, there are three groups of people in your world to contact. The first is made up of individuals who have direct experience in, or knowledge of, the industry or field in which you're seeking employment. Regardless of their respective positions, these individuals have inside knowledge that can be very valuable.

Think about all the people you know. Consider past employers, relatives, co-workers, church members, and neighbors. Who do you know that fits into this first category? Write down the names of three people to contact:

I could contact:

1.

2.

3.

You can expand this list later. We just want to get you started.

A second group to contact includes individuals who, though not directly involved in the type of work you're pursuing, tend to know a lot of people. These folks are constantly making contact with a wide variety of people. Some of your best contacts will come from these "walking encyclopedias." They may include dentists, grocers, Aunt Laura, a college roommate, and your aerobics instructor. Now list three such individuals from this category whom you could contact:

1.

2.

3.

You probably know more people than you might think. The key to making progress is to start asking the right people for the right kind of assistance. Why do you need this type of help? Because you have a tremendous investment to make as a potential employee. Don't forget that you're of great value. Asking for assistance is a strength, because in effect you're saying, "I am worth helping."

There is a third group of contacts you should pursue. Those are acquaintances who don't fit into the two previous groups, but who may know someone who could help. You could overlook such people because they have no obvious connection to your job objective. Maybe your neighbor has a cousin who hires for the very position you seek! Your newspaper carrier's mother could be employed for an organization you'd like to contact. Mine these contacts for leads, and you'll be surprised at the treasure you'll uncover. Below list five individuals to contact.

1.

2.

3.

4.

5.

By accessing people from these three groups, you'll be able to target hiring managers to contact. On the average, you have the potential to generate 250 names from these three groups. We suggest you identify your 50 best contacts and start networking with them to identify hiring managers.

Once you know who to contact, what do you say when you call? Knowing how to request reasonable assistance from your contacts is important. Marketing #4 is filled with helpful tips, and examples of how to go to these individuals for additional contacts.

Turn to page 49 and read through Marketing #4, "Networking to Identify Hiring Managers."

Welcome Back!

Is there a more direct approach to networking than using the phone?

Is it possible to identify potential hiring managers without calling friends and acquaintances? There is. But before trying another strategy, remember that the benefit of accessing your current relationships is the trust level generated between you and the hiring manager to whom you're referred. It makes sense: Aren't you more comfortable going to dentists, doctors, or hair dressers who are recommended by people you know? A hiring manager is no different. He or she is more likely to consider you as a potential employee because you have a mutual, respected friend.

STRENGTH IN NUMBERS

MEN CAN DO JOINTLY WHAT THEY CANNOT DO SINGLY; AND THE UNION OF MINDS AND HANDS, THE CONCENTRATION OF THEIR POWER, BECOMES ALMOST OMNIPOTENT.

DANIEL WEBSTER

Take the time to farm your field of contacts first. However, if 50 organizations in your area are hiring for the position you seek, and your contacts have only led you to the managers of ten of these organizations, then how do you reach the remaining 40?

You need a second strategy. You need to identify the appropriate hiring manager by making direct contact with companies/organizations.

With a little effort you can identify these additional 40 hiring managers and contact them in a diplomatic, appropriate way. In Marketing #5, you'll learn an effective approach for expanding your list of potential hiring managers through direct contact.

Turn to page 51 and complete Marketing #5, "Identifying Hiring Managers Through Direct Contact."

Welcome Back!

Let's briefly review where we are. We started out this section on R&R interviewing by saying that the key to selling a product is getting it in front of potential buyers. When applied to the job search, this means that your primary task in looking for work is to get the product —you— in front of potential buyers—hiring managers. You then saw how R&R interviewing is the best strategy for exposing yourself to these managers.

Next, you learned how to identify these potential hiring managers by:

1. Networking through current friends and acquaintances

2. Making direct contact with organizations

Step #2: Contacting Potential Hiring Managers

Once you've identified the hiring manager for the position you're pursuing, there are three ways to contact him or her.

The first way is in person. Another name for this approach is "cold calling." It means walking into an organization without any previous introduction and asking to speak with the hiring manager. The challenge in cold calling is to initiate a conversation that results in an immediate appointment. If you've been referred to this individual by a mutual acquaintance, the conversation might go something like this:

You: "Good morning, I'm here to speak with Jim Gray."

Secretary/receptionist: "Do you have an appointment?"

You: "No, but an associate of Jim's suggested I stop by and introduce myself. I'll only take a few minutes. Could you tell Mr. Gray I'm here?"

Secretary/receptionist: "One moment, please. I'll see if Mr. Gray is available."

To use this approach effectively you need to have a confident and commanding presence. You must also be able to think on your feet. Cold calling is most successful when you're pursuing a position that requires assertive character qualities such as sales, marketing, or promotion. In these situations, you're already demonstrating some initial aptitude for the field or industry. Avoid cold calling in very conservative or transitional organizations where this approach might come off as unprofessional or abrasive.

A second way to contact a potential hiring manager is by phone. The telephone can be an excellent tool for setting up an R&R interview. It's less time-consuming than an in-person contact, but still provides direct communication with the hiring manager. In Marketing #6 you'll learn how to make successful direct contact by phone.

Turn to page 52 and complete Marketing #6, "Contacting Hiring Managers by Phone."

Welcome Back!

The introductory letter is a third effective way of setting up a referral interview. And it has two major advantages:

1. A letter goes directly to your contact. You eliminate the work of going through a secretary to make initial contact.

2. A letter paves the way when you phone to make the actual appointment; you've already established contact with the hiring manager. This gives you more leverage with a secretary. If you're asked about the nature of the call, you can say, "I'm following up with the hiring manager to see if she received the information I sent."

In Marketing #7, you'll learn how to put together an effective letter of introduction.

Turn to page 53 and complete Marketing #7, "Contacting the Hiring Manager by Letter."

Welcome Back!

Once you've succeeded in getting a 30-minute appointment with the hiring manager, you need to make the most of this time. And since you initiated the contact, it's up to you to structure the half hour.

Step #3: Conducting the R&R Interview

To maximize your appointment you must consider what you want to get out of the interview. Essentially, you'll want to seek a goal. You'll want the hiring manager to:

1. Like you.
2. See your potential.
3. Offer suggestions for improving your presentation (resume, appearance, communication, etc.).
4. Refer you to other hiring managers who may have an interest in you.

How can you achieve these goals? Here are some solid suggestions:

First, you can make a favorable impression on the hiring managers by giving them the chance to talk about their own career. Simply ask how they got into the field, and what part of the job is most enjoyable. Give managers a chance to share their own career story. By learning how they got where they are, you may find some common ground. Similar backgrounds are a natural way to build relationships.

A second strategy is to compliment the manager in some aspect of the company, department, or service. A genuine compliment is another great relationship builder.

Third, find a point of common interest. Look for clues in the manager's office. Magazines, pictures, trophies can become targets for building common ground. Don't hesitate to use them.

Fourth, there's the factor of "chemistry" (i.e. personality, natural attraction) that, if present, will cause you to make a favorable impression.

OUT OF CONTROL

"WHY IS IT THAT SOMEONE ELSE GOT THE JOB, AND NOT ME?" IF YOU'VE EVER BEEN BEAT OUT FOR A POSITION, THEN TAKE HEART. THE OTHER PERSON MAY HAVE GOTTEN THE JOB DUE TO ONE OF THREE THINGS WHICH NO ONE HAS CONTROL OVER WHEN IT COMES TO GETTING WORK: TIMING, HIRING TRENDS, AND THE BIASES OF HIRING MANAGERS. THINK, SOONER OR LATER, ONE OF THESE IS BOUND TO WORK IN YOUR FAVOR.

The hiring manager will see your potential if you show him or her a well-written resume. It's also good to ask the manager to share perceptions of the qualifications needed for the position you are pursuing. Then, demonstrate how you meet these qualfications.

The hiring manager will give you suggestions for improving your job search if you ask for ways you could be better prepared and how you could improve your personal presentation.

The hiring manager will refer you to other hiring managers if he or she has no immediate openings but believes you could be a valuable employee. The manager may know someone else who is hiring and may genuinely enjoy helping others (including you!) find a satisfying job.

Is it possible to reach these outcomes in a brief 30-minute appointment with a potential hiring manager? Yes. Marketing #8 will give you a more complete guideline for conducting an R&R interview.

Turn to page 60 and read through Marketing #8, "Conducting a Referral Interview."

Welcome Back!

After reading through the previous interview, you may feel ready to charge out into the marketplace to start conducting a slew of interviews. On the other hand you may be thinking, "There's no way I can conduct an interview like this."

Remember, this dialog is just a sample. Don't be intimidated. Regardless of how uncomfortable you may feel with R&R interviewing, you can do it. Practice if you have to. Find some friends or acquaintances who are hiring managers and ask them to role play an interview. The more experience you get, the more comfortable you'll feel.

Be yourself, develop your own style, seek to reach the basic goals suggested in this section, and you'll do fine!

Some final tips:

1. Arrive ten minutes early for your appointment. This gives you time for any last-minute preparation or unexpected delays.
2. Look sharp. Your interviewer could be a potential employer; so dress appropriately. If in doubt, make an advance trip to the organization and observe how the employees dress.
3. Be sure to have extra copies of your resume.

ON THE FACE OF IT

SUCCESSFUL PEOPLE SMILE A LOT.

ANONYMOUS

4. Be prepared. Know why you're visiting this person. Think about how the hiring manager can best help you. Write out your agenda and questions on a 3×5 card to use as a reference during the interview. List five questions you'd like the hiring manager to

answer. Also, write down five strengths you want to communicate about yourself.

5. As much as possible, stick within the time frame you agreed upon. Usually this will be 20 to 30 minutes. If the manager wants to spend more time with you, fine, but be sure it's his or her decision.

6. If the manager raises concerns about your potential, be sure to have a response that resolves these questions during the interview.

7. When someone gives you a referral, be sure you have permission to use his or her name as the referral source. Also, gather as much information about contacting the referral as seems appropriate. This will include a job title and phone number.

8. After the interview, take a few minutes to review what you did and didn't learn. Jot down suggestions for future interviews; learn from each encounter.

R&R Interviews: Saying "Thanks"

After every interview, it's wise to send a thank-you note. This can be handwritten, or typed. Make it brief and complimentary.

The purpose of the thank-you note is twofold. First, and most importantly, it's a basic courtesy. Whether or not your interview was profitable, the manager did commit valuable time to you. This merits a written appreciation.

Second, a thank-you note reinforces your name and leaves another favorable impression of you with the hiring manager. Remember, getting a job means building positive relationships. A thank-you note is another step in that direction.

For samples of effective thank-you notes, turn to pages 78-83.

On the average, you'll receive one job interview for every 25 R&R interviews you conduct. This means you should expect to talk to a number of hiring managers and be able to walk away with no definite employment prospects. Don't be discouraged. Every time this happens you're still one step closer to a job interview. In addition, you're also gaining valuable information and skills from your contacts. By penetrating the job market, you're taking an active role in finding work. No longer do you have to sit around waiting, getting discouraged, losing perspective, and eventually giving up.

Make R&R interviewing the cornerstone of your job search.

Other Job-Finding Strategies

You've just looked at the most effective strategy available for uncovering job opportunities—R&R interviewing. However, there are other effective approaches to use. Depending upon your particular situation, some will be more helpful than others.

1. Join professional organizations, attend regional or national conferences.

This approach helps you to position yourself to make contact with others in the field. Many relationships and job leads are concentrated in professional settings. Here's a true story:

John was in public relations, but considering a change. While attending a monthly luncheon of fellow professionals, John sat next to Bill, the owner of a small multimedia business. During the course of their conversation, John learned that Bill was expanding his company and looking for someone with John's background and interest. Two weeks later John was working for Bill in a challenging new position.

The moral of the story: "Position yourself for opportunity."

2. Identify ten organizations for which you'd like to work.

Find out how they publicize their openings—phone hotlines, weekly postings, public advertisement, etc. Also, find out how frequently job postings are updated. (Usually it's weekly.) Check regularly with these organizations to identify potential jobs. When possible, show up in person to look at openings. Make friends with the employees. Your visibility and persistence can give you an edge.

Here's what can happen when you put these tips to work: Susan wanted to work for a company called Compton Industries. Every Monday morning, she would visit the personnel office, look at job listings, and chat briefly with the staff. Within a few weeks Susan was on a first-name basis with most of the personnel staff. Impressed with her enthusiasm and persistence, the head of the department staff called Susan for an initial interview the moment a position opened that fit her qualifications.

The moral of the story: "Persistence pays off."

BURIED TREASURE

OPPORTUNITIES ARE USUALLY DISGUISED AS HARD WORK, SO MOST PEOPLE DON'T RECOGNIZE THEM.

ANN LANDERS

3. Become familiar with the needs and problems of a particular organization or department. Then present a proposal of how you could address the particular issue. Here's another true story of how a principle was put into practice.

In sharing his job interests with a friend, Fred learned about a small organization that matched his skills. Interested, Fred became more acquainted with the organization. And his friend gave him the name of an employee who was familiar with the area Fred was interested in.

After talking with this person, Fred outlined a general proposal addressing a current service need. He then contacted the organization's director, explained his purpose in calling, and asked for an opportunity to present his proposal.

The director was obviously interested and met with Fred. Their meeting led to other sessions in which the director and Fred hammered out a more specific approach to Fred's proposal.

Eventually, a position was created, and Fred was hired to implement his plan.

The moral of the story: "Find a way to help an employer make money, save money, and eliminate problems, and you'll find a job."

4. Before you respond to job listings and help wanted ads, take time to find out more specifics about the position. Consider one person who knew what to do:

Mary saw a position in the newspaper that interested her. The advertisement said to send a resume and gave the name and address of the organization.

Before responding, Mary called the company and asked to speak with the person hiring for this position. When asked about the purpose of her call, Mary said she was considering applying for the job, but had a few questions to ask the hiring manager before she could make a decision.

Mary was put in touch with the hiring manager. Mary then explained briefly her interest in the position, but expressed a need for more information to determine if she'd be a serious candidate for the job. Mary found out this was a new position. She also learned what the manager was looking for in an employee, and how well her background matched the position.

After gathering all her new information, Mary confidently said she'd like to pursue the job and asked the manager for an opportunity to meet and discuss the position and her background in more detail. The manager consented.

Armed with a knowledge of what the manager wanted, Mary tailored a resume specifically for the position. Her extra efforts turned a newspaper ad into a job interview. She had gained a decisive edge on the competition.

Moral of the story: "Those who go the extra mile may actually be taking a shortcut."

5. Regularly check resources for job leads. These might include professional publications, alumni offices, state employment security job banks, recruiting firms (for jobs over $40,000), and employment agencies (you pay fee).

The idea here is to keep as many irons in the fire as possible. Depending upon your situation, some of these resources will be better than others. However, none of the above should replace R&R interviews as your primary job search strategy.

6. Don't forget Intercristo. We list 35,000 jobs in a variety of ministry-related areas in the U.S. and abroad. If you're considering working in a Christian organization, our Intermatch service can put you in touch with current job openings.

Call toll free: 1-800-426-1342.

Intercristo's **Tentmakers International** also provides listings of secular work opportunities overseas. A secular job in a foreign country may be the vehicle you need to be involved in overseas ministry. For Tentmakers International call 1-800-251-7739.

GOT A MATCH?

IN 1984, OVER 85,000 PEOPLE INQUIRED ABOUT INTERCRISTO'S INTERMATCH SERVICE THAT MATCHES CHRISTIANS WITH CURRENT CAREER OPPORTUNITIES IN THE WORLD. OVER 700 MEN AND WOMEN WERE PLACED IN JOBS THAT MATCHED THEIR CAREER DESIRES AND GOD GIVEN ABILITIES.

Let us help you expand your knowledge of employment opportunities both in the U.S. and abroad.

Moral of the story: "If you place your product in front of enough potential buyers, you're bound to make a sale."

The committed job seeker must pass through two more steps before closing a sale. Both are discussed in Step #7, the last phase in the process of marketing yourself.

STEP #7:

Getting the Job

The process of actually getting a job comes down to one basic principle: a discussion or series of discussions between you and a hiring manager that has one of two results—either you're offered a job or you receive a call or letter saying "Sorry but you were not selected."

All of your work in the previous chapters on assessment, exploration, and marketing is geared towards these last two vital tasks—getting the job offer and accepting the job offer.

To succeed in these tasks you must become skilled in two areas—interviewing for a job and negotiating a job offer.

All of the effort you've expended to this point will be of little value if you're unable to succeed in these two areas. If you have had trouble turning job interviews into job offers, then read carefully through the section on interviewing. If you have never taken an active role in determining what you're worth to an employer, pay close attention to the information you'll find in the section on "Negotiating a Job Offer." You're now ready to put the final touches on your marketing effort.

Interviewing for a Job:

Volumes have been written about job interviews. No other part of the job search process has received the attention, analysis, and print that's been given to job interviewing. Every book has a different angle, technique, or approach guaranteed to help you win, sell, empower, overcome, and take charge! Who's right? What do you really need to know to get the job?

Our goal in Career Kit has been to give you the essentials you need to know for meaningful career direction. With this objective in mind, we want to suggest eight principles that best summarize what you need to know about job interviews:

1. A job interview is a predictable encounter involving basic expectations and rules of conduct.

2. Preparation will improve your effectiveness in a job interview.

3. The hiring manager has much more at stake in the interview than you.

4. Successful job interviewers know how to uncover and address positively the needs, concerns, and expectations of the hiring manager.

5. Most hiring decisions are based more on intangibles — intuition, good feelings, like-mindedness, etc. — than on tangibles — qualfications, experience, and training.

6. Effective interviewers learn how to tell the "best truth" about themselves.

7. No two interviews are alike. Presenting yourself in a way that's appropriate is more important than being right, clever, funny, or even qualified.

8. What happens after the interview can make the difference in getting the job.

Now, let's take a closer look at each of these principles.

1. A job interview is a predictable encounter involving basic expectations and rules of conduct.

You don't have to walk into a job interview without any idea of what to expect. Although each interview situation is different, you need to consider some fundamental expectations. We call them "interview dynamics." Essentially, an interview is a two-way discussion that focuses on a special agenda. Your agenda and the hiring manager's agenda are illustrated on next page.

INTERVIEWING DYNAMICS

You

- What Do We Have In Common
- What are His/Her Needs or Concerns
- How Can I Demonstrate My Ability To Contribute
- What Questions Do I Need Answered
- Do I Want The Job

Hiring Manager

- Do I Like Her/Him
- Does She/He Want the Job
- Can She/He Do The Job
- Will She/He Fit In
- What Risks In Hiring

An effective, successful interview is one in which both you and the hiring manager can get your agendas on the table for discussion. You should anticipate the hiring manager's agenda and walk into the interview with an idea of how you'll respond to his or her needs and concerns.

In addition to these basic expectations, there are also rules of conduct that go into a successful interview experience. Here then are the Ten Commandments of Conduct:

1. Arrive alone, and be on time. Give yourself a few minutes to relax and get ready for the interview.

2. Dress appropriately and be well groomed. Keep perfume, jewelry, and makeup to a minimum.

3. Address the interviewer as "Mr." or "Ms." unless you are instructed otherwise.

4. Wait for the interviewer to offer a handshake and/or a seat.

5. Avoid arguing, debating with, or correcting the interviewer.

6. Keep your responses between 30 and 90 seconds in length.

7. Avoid asking about money and benefits (your interests) until you have a job offer.

8. Never lie. Learn how to tell the best truth about yourself (see page 33).

NEVER TELL A LIE

ALWAYS TELL THE TRUTH. I DON'T HAVE A GOOD ENOUGH MEMORY TO BE A LIAR.

THEODORE ROOSEVELT

9. Don't focus on your weaknesses, insecurities, and doubts. The purpose of an interview is not to seek acceptance, it's to demonstrate your value and potential.

10. Lastly, if you're interested in the position, say so. This is no time to hide your feelings.

Follow this code of conduct, and your interview performance is bound to improve.

2. Preparation will improve your effectiveness in a job interview.

The old adage that "planning precedes performance" certainly applies to a job interview. By investing time and energy in preparation for an interview, you develop an edge over other candidates, and you may maximize the limited amount of time you have in the actual interview. Good interview preparation is based on the following six points.

1. Ask for a job description. If none is available, talk with the hiring manager to find out what he or she sees as the essential qualifications and strengths required for the job.

2. Tailor your resume to the specific position you seek.

3. Find out as much as you can about the company/department—its products, services, needs, or problems. This becomes an increasingly important factor the higher up you move in an organization. Keep these basic sources of information in mind:

- Library resources, such as Standard and Poors Register of Corporations, if it's a publicly held company.
- Company brochures and other publicity pieces. Contact the public relations or marketing department if it's a large company.
- Competitors. Talk with a person in a similar area at a competing firm. As a rule, competitors make it a point to know the strengths and weaknesses of others in the marketplace.
- Talk with other employees in the organization. Network to see if you know a person who knows someone in the company. Ask if you could buy him or her lunch just to learn a little bit about the group. If you try this approach, keep your questions general—don't probe.
- Talk with customers/recipients of the organization's products or services.

4. Anticipate an employer's concerns about your experience, training, work history, age, and formulate a short positive response to each concern.

5. Develop a list of at least ten promotional statements you can use to highlight strengths and demonstrate your potential. Write them out and commit each to memory. Practice saying them to another person. Be sure you can maintain eye contact while talking positively and confidently about yourself.

6. Be sure you know who'll be conducting the interview. If in doubt, call the organization and ask. When you're given a name, ask if this individual will be making the hiring decision.

Getting these answers will help you avoid feeling let down, if for instance you will be interviewing with three people instead of one or if you expect to meet the hiring manager and find out this is a routine screening interview with personnel.

3. The hiring manager has much more at stake in the interview than you.

Think of it: you walk into a job interview with no offer or position in the company/department (unless of course, you already work there). What's the worst thing that can happen to you? That's right, you walk out of the interview in the same condition in which you entered. In a job interview, you have nothing to lose, and everything to gain.

Hiring managers, however, are in a different situation. They have work that isn't getting done because a position is vacant. They must put in extra time and effort to find an employee. Hiring someone is more work in addition to their regular duties. For most managers, it's no fun.

Hiring people is hard, risky business. The hiring manager has a lot at stake. He needs help to make a good decision. Your task, initially in the interview, should be to help this anxious, concerned, overloaded individual make a good decision. When you start focusing primarily on the employer's needs, and not your own, job interviews will likely turn into job offers.

4. Successful job interviewers know how to uncover and address positively the needs, concerns, and expectations of the hiring manager.

Your primary mission in an interview is to identify the employer's needs and address, positively, your ability to meet those needs. The strengths and experience you possess are only significant as they relate to what that hiring manager is looking for. You may have outstanding credentials, but if the manager is looking for a team player, you need to address your ability to work with a team. You may be prepared to wax eloquent on how well you fit the job description. But if the manager has a particular problem he needs to solve with a new employee, then it's up to you to identify that problem and address it.

YOUR NEEDS, OR MINE

I'LL TELL YOU WHY I WANT THIS JOB. I THRIVE ON CHALLENGES. I LIKE BEING STRETCHED TO MY FULL CAPACITY. I LIKE SOLVING PROBLEMS. ALSO, MY CAR IS ABOUT TO BE REPOSSESSED.

JOB INTERVIEW

It's like any purchase decision. When you go to buy a car, naturally you want to buy a model that will meet your needs. If you're concerned about gas mileage, why care about a discount if the auto gets only ten miles per gallon? The hiring manager wants to fulfill his need. The question is, are you the person who can meet it?

How do you know what a hiring manager is looking for in an employee? You don't, unless he tells you. Take the time to identify the manager's needs, problems, or concerns early in the interview. You'll find this step critical to your success in getting a job offer.

Note: As a general rule, when two people talk, the one who feels the best about the discussion is usually the person who does the most talking. What implications does that hold for a job interview? The more you can get a hiring manager to share needs, expectations, and problems, the better he or she will feel about your time together.

5. Most hiring decisions are based more on intangibles than tangibles.

It was obvious to the director that Bill was much more qualified for the job than Mary. However, there seemed to be an instant rapport with Mary. The director felt comfortable with her. And in the end, Mary got the job offer. "Does this happen often?" Yes, every day!

Success in a job interview is as dependent on the chemistry between two people as it is qualifications. If you find common ground with the hiring manager and develop a natural rapport during the interview, you stand a good chance of getting the job offer.

Look to establish common ground as you go into an interview. Areas to pursue might include hobbies, professional interests, lifestyle similarities (single, married, kids), places of birth, education, or vacationing. Any of these areas can be a vital part of building a bridge of trust, interest, and appeal with the hiring manager.

Compliments also build relationships. Mentioning the kind secretary, beautiful facilities, excellent reputation, or solid track record of the company or hiring manager can make all the difference in an interview. Few things are more appealing to a person than a sincere, tasteful compliment. Be affirming, but don't overdo it.

Try to align yourself with the needs, values, interests, and concerns of the hiring manager, because these are the factors that will ultimately influence your chances of a job offer.

6. Effective interviewers learn how to tell the "best truth" about themselves.

The old adage, "It's not what you say, but how you say it" certainly applies to the job interview. Too many people annoy potential employers because they don't know how to state accurate information in an appealing, positive way.

An interview is no time to lie or exaggerate the truth about your background or experience. However, it is an opportunity for sharing the best parts of who you are. This is what we mean by telling the "best truth" about yourself.

Consider the information you share in an interview from the perspective of a eulogy. Think about the last funeral you attended. Remember the eulogies for Uncle Fred or Cousin Cathy? What were people saying? Did they talk about Fred's abrasive personality or did they stress his willingness to speak his mind? Was Cathy remembered as someone who "needed to be liked," or was she praised for "her ability to get along with just about anyone?" Who brought up Sue's instability? All the Rev. Jones said was that Sue "always chose to risk and meet life head on. Her life was anything but dull."

Why do people talk this way at funerals? Are they avoiding the truth? No. They are simply telling the best truth about the deceased, because memorial services are a time to remember the best.

In this way, job interviews and funerals are similar. If you want to leave a positive, lasting impression in the mind of the hiring manager, then learn how to tell the best truth about yourself.

What difference can telling the best truth make in an interview? You decide after you read the following examples.

Interviewer's question: "Why did you leave your last job?"
Your response:
Worst truth: "My boss and I just couldn't get along."
Best truth: "Although successful in my job, I decided to pursue a better work opportunity such as this position offers."

Interviewer's question: "Is it true that you have held three different jobs in the past four years?"
Your response:
Worst Truth: "That's right, each job turned out to be different from what I expected."
Best Truth: "Yes, I know how to go after something I want. It's taken me three jobs to figure out what I should be pursuing. I'm relieved to have the confusion now behind me."

Interviewer's question: "What are some of your weaknesses?"
Your response:
Worst truth: "I tend to be a little disorganized."
Best truth: "I am so responsive to customer needs that sometimes my own paperwork gets postponed until I schedule a block of time to catch up and organize."

Do you see the difference in these responses? Depending on how you present yourself, your conversation is either selling lemons or lemonade. Work at telling the best truth about yourself!

7. No two interviews are alike. Presenting yourself in a way that's appropriate is more important than being right, clever, funny, or even qualified!

Jim was bright, experienced, articulate, and confident. He had done his homework and was ready for the interview. At the start of the interview, he told a funny story that had been well received at a previous interview. Unfortunately, the hiring manager was a very serious, conservative individual. Jim's joke fell on deaf ears, and so did his best effort to sell himself as a job candidate.

Jim learned his lesson the hard way. What's appropriate in an interview depends on who's sitting across from you. A quiet, reserved hiring manager will probably be more direct and to the point. A verbal, expressive manager will look for energy and lively discussion. The traditional manager will expect propriety and formality. And the manager who values reserved relationships will look for warmth and sensitivity.

Find out what kind of person the hiring manager is prior to the interview, and you'll have a definite advantage. You can gear your presentation to his or her style. If this isn't possible, then you must go in with wide eyes and open ears. Look for clues and cues, like office decor, personal dress, seating arrangement, level of organization, topics of conversation, and the general flow of conversation. Go into the interview prepared, but be ready to adapt your approach and responses to the individual you meet.

NUMBER ONE INTERVIEW QUESTION

THE MOST COMMON QUESTION THAT'S PROBABLY ASKED IN 90 PERCENT OF ALL INTERVIEWS IS, "TELL ME ABOUT YOURSELF," WHICH CAN BE ASKED IN MANY WAYS; "WHAT'S YOUR BACKGROUND?," "WHAT DO YOU DO?," "WHY ARE YOU HERE?," "WHAT CAN YOU BRING TO MY COMPANY?," IT'S ALL THE SAME QUESTION.

JAMES CHALLENGER

8. What happens after the interview can make the difference in getting the job.

After her interview was over, Chris took the time to send a thank-you note to Ms. Miller, the hiring manager. She mailed her letter the same day of the interview. Very briefly, Chris thanked Ms. Miller for the information and conversation. She stated how she could meet Ms. Miller's needs, and reaffirmed her interest in the position.

Two days later Chris was hired for the position. After a week on the job, Chris asked Ms. Miller if she would mind sharing what influenced her hiring decision. Ms. Miller said it was the thank-you note.

In work, as in all of life, it's the little things that often count. A thank-you note communicates courtesy, follow-through, and interest. It serves to remind the hiring manager of your name and potential. Smart job-seekers make it a point to add this final touch. Your thank-you note should be personally addressed, easy to read, and brief.

Turn to pages 78-83 for samples of effective thank-you notes.

Negotiating the Job Offer

There are three times in life when you should expect to negotiate for what you want:

1. When you buy or sell a car

2. When you buy or sell a house

3. When you accept or leave a job.

What do each of these three transactions have in common? They all involve commodities which, depending upon the individuals, can represent a wide range of perceived value. That's why each transaction must be negotiated. All negotiation serves two purposes:

1. To find a mutually acceptable point of perceived value.

2. To provide both buyer and seller with a sense of success and victory in the transaction.

When you neglect to negotiate a job offer, you lose on two counts. First, you lose monetarily. A good employer is no different from you. He or she wants a good buy. That means getting a good product at the lowest possible price. It only makes sense to offer you a low figure. If you accept, then the employer's just made an incredible buy.

Remember, most salary increases are based upon where you start. It's easier to get a significant increase in salary before, instead of after, you're hired. Once you're already on board, your bargaining leverage is not as great.

Second, failure to negotiate means you lose emotionally. You forfeit your right to assert your value. You lose the privilege of finding out that an employer values you enough to pay a little more than he or she may have wished to get you.

Though employment negotiation can be a complex process, there are some fundamental questions everyone must address.

What is negotiable in a job offer? Although the salary is the main negotiable item, there are other things up for discussion. These might include vacation time, health benefits, professional development opportunity, starting date, retirement benefits, and possible moving expenses.

When do I negotiate? Salary negotiations shouldn't start until you have a clear offer from the employer. This can be either verbal, or in writing. But it must be clear. Until you have an offer extended to you, avoid discussing benefits, compensation, starting dates, etc.

If you're asked what kind of money you're looking for, respond by asking about the salary range for the position. Once this is stated ($8 - $10/hour, $1200 - 1350/month, or $38,000 - 45,000/year), respond by quoting the high end of the range as an acceptable amount ($10/hour, $1350/month or $45,000/year). If you're asked how much money you were making on your last job, don't lie. Either state the salary range for the position or say something to the effect that: "I was making $ amount in my last/current position. One of my reasons for pursuing other alternatives is that I feel I'm not being adequately compensated for my contribution."

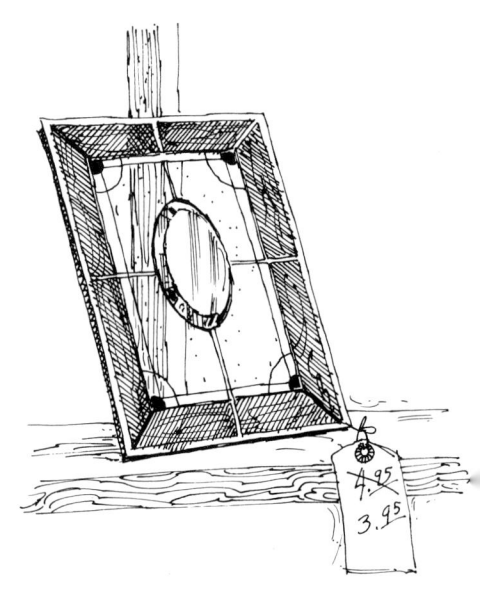

The same principles apply when negotiating for benefits, moving expenses, etc. When you bring these items up for discussion prior to a job offer, you put your interests ahead of the employer's. This is not what you want to communicate in an interview.

How Do I Negotiate? Successful negotiation between you and a potential employer is built upon several important conditions.

1. You possess a genuine level of interest in the job offer. It's a compliment to be offered a job. The hiring manager wants to know you appreciate this action and desire to pursue the possibility further. Be sure you communicate this appreciation in your initial response.

2. You have a knowledge of all the pertinent facts. If the hiring manager has not clearly communicated what's being offered to you (benefits, salary, starting date, etc.), then it's perfectly legitimate for you to ask about these specifics. Gather all the facts before you make any decision.

PERK UP!

PERKS HAVE BECOME A STAPLE OF THE CORPORATE WORLD...

ONE FEMALE EXECUTIVE WHO SAID SHE HAD TO DO A LOT OF SOCIALIZING AS PART OF HER BUSINESS, GOT ALL OF HER LAUNDRY BILLS PAID BY HER COMPANY.

ONE MANUFACTURING EXECUTIVE, WHO WAS ASSIGNED TO A SUBSIDIARY AN HOUR'S DRIVE FROM HIS HOME, GOT HELICOPTER TRANSPORTATION TO AND FROM WORK EVERY DAY.

ONE COMPANY USED TO LEASE A SALMON STREAM IN ICELAND FOR FISHING USE BY ITS SENIOR EXECUTIVES AND THEIR GUESTS, BUT HAS STOPPED THE PRACTICE. ("HUNTING LODGES WERE PRETTY POPULAR A NUMBER OF YEARS AGO," SAID ONE BUSINESS CONSULTANT, "BUT THEY'VE FALLEN OUT OF FAVOR, BECAUSE THEY ARE A LITTLE HARD TO JUSTIFY.")

BOB GREENE

3. You have enough time to thoughtfully consider the offer. You shouldn't be pressured to respond to an offer during the interview. It's entirely reasonable to ask a potential employer for time to consider his or her offer.

Suggest a specific time when you'll communicate your decision. This, too, may need to be negotiated with the employer. Don't string out the decision so long that the employer begins to suspect your interest level. If this happens, you'll probably lose the offer.

For most positions a few days to one week should be sufficient. If you have a few pending interviews and want to postpone making a decision, explain this to the employer and explore a reasonable time when you can announce your decision.

If you're not satisfied with the offer, you must confidently communicate your interest in the position, and your ability to contribute. Once doing this, candidly communicate that you can't accept the offer as it stands.

If salary is the issue, and you're asked what would be acceptable, ask for 10 - 15% more than you expect to get. Remember, the manager must be able to negotiate down if he or she is to have a sense of success and victory in the offer. Give him or her this opportunity to bargain.

If any future arrangements for salary increases, additional vacation, special bonuses are communicated during the job offer, then inquire whether these are standard policy or special arrangements. If they aren't standard policy, then ask for the employer's commitments in writing.

Factors to Consider Before You Negotiate

Before you ever sit down with a prospective employer, there are several important things you need to keep in mind:

1. Know your market value.

Ted had never made more than $18,000 a year. He had just completed his MBA when he was interviewed for a new job. Asked what kind of money he needed, Ted didn't inquire about the salary range. He simply decided he needed more than he was making. So Ted said $20,000.

Ted failed to get the job. The reason was that no one in the firm was making under $25,000. Ted's income request communicated he didn't know his own market or his value.

Sue was making a major career change. Well paid in her previous job, she pursued a new career with enthusiasm. After five interviews and no job offers, Sue realized she had overestimated her worth. In her new field, Sue's experience and training did not carry the same price tag she was used to. Sue didn't know her market value for her new career.

TOO MUCH, TOO SOON

"LET'S TALK SALARY. HOW DOES 'ASTRONOMICAL' SOUND TO YOU?"

CANDIDATE IN INTERVIEW

Like Ted and Sue, you must reconcile your own gifts, background, and experience to the marketplace. To negotiate effectively, you must know your true market value. Determining the income range offered for a position should have been a part of your informational interview process. If you didn't ask the salary range for the position you're pursuing, then conduct a few interviews to find out what people are making in similar jobs. You might also contact others doing similar work. Share your background and experience, and ask them to suggest a reasonable income level.

If you're considering an offer in a different part of the country, be aware of cost-of-living factors. Remember, a dollar will stretch further in Fort Wayne, Indiana than it will in Los Angeles, California.

The bottom line is don't try to negotiate in a vacuum; know your market value.

2. Consider the competition.

Jean interviewed for a highly competitive entry-level position. In an effort to buy time to complete another interesting interview, she asked for a week to consider the first offer.

When she called back, the position was filled. When the competition is high and your leverage is minimal, be ready to make the play when the ball is in your court.

3. Size up the company/organization.

As a general rule, the larger the organization, the more standardized the compensation schedules for most employees. If you receive a job offer from a "bureaucracy," then expect to negotiate within its set limits. If you receive an offer from a smaller organization, expect to have more freedom negotiating the terms of your employment.

4. Read the hiring manager.

Most of us are willing to pay more for something we really want. Hiring managers are no different. If the manager really wants you, he or she will pay more to get you. You can tell this when:

• At or immediately following the interview, you're offered the job.

• The manager has spent significant time getting to know you, exposing you to the organization, calling you back with additional questions. When the offer is finally made, you can be sure you are the one he or she wants. Here, you're in a good position to negotiate.

• You get introduced to the other players on the team. If a manager begins to think you're the one, he or she will frequently take you around and have you meet other co-workers. When you start "meeting the family," recognize that you have become a strong candidate.

• You're becoming a confidant. If a manager starts sharing inside information with you (needs, problems, new direction), a major step has been taken. You've gained his or her trust and respect. This is another indicator of strong interest in you as a candidate.

5. Evaluate your ego.

For better or worse, what an employer offers to you is an indication of perceived value. Your response to an offer can get tied up with your ego. If you're feeling unappreciated and receive a low salary offer, it's easy to become indignant, disgusted, and even demanding in making a counter offer to the manager. An emotionally-charged response in this situation will send "red flags" to the manager about what working with you will be like.

Offering you the position may be an emotional decision for the manager, but offering you more money will be a rational decision. Don't respond emotionally to a salary offer. Keep cool and present a logical case for why you should receive higher compensation. By the way, the discussion should focus more on the employer's needs than yours. If you're at a loss for rationale, you can rely on the most fundamental, logical argument around: "Because I'm worth it!"

On the other hand, you may be confident, self-assured, qualified, and likeable, yet still receive a low job offer. In this case, it is possible that your ego has gotten in the way of the negotiation. In other words, you considered yourself such an outstanding candidate that you didn't work as hard at demonstrating your value. If this happens, tell the manager that, based on your qualifications, you had expected a better offer. Then ask for his or her own perceptions of your qualifications. This gives you an opportunity to reinforce your strong background by addressing specific areas of concern to the manager. If you do this successfully, you enhance your perceived value along with your chances for negotiating a better offer.

When NOT to Negotiate?

You don't always need to negotiate a job offer. In certain situations negotiating is neither appropriate nor possible. Generally speaking, it's not wise to push for negotiation in the following situations:

1. When an employer has made you a very reasonable and fair job offer. Some employers will do all they can to be fair and make an offer up front. If you're interviewing with such a person and start haggling about salary, or vacation, you stand a good chance of insulting the employer and losing the job.

2. When you're pursuing employment in a field or industry that has a fixed scale or salary structure. Many government and union jobs fit into this category.

3. When your qualifications for the position are minimal and it's obvious that the employer is giving you a great opportunity. If you're just breaking into a field, desperately in need of work experience, and can live with the compensation offered, then it might be wise to worry less about padding your pocketbook and instead concentrate on taking the job and building your credentials.

4. When you're in need of immediate employment and can't afford to risk losing the offer by choosing to negotiate with the employer.

5. When you're in a glutted field and, although your background should cause you to be worth more, the law of supply and demand is not in your favor. If you don't take the job as offered, the employer has more fish in the sea.

When an offer isn't:

What should you do if you get a "Dear John" call or letter instead of a job offer? Shake the dust off your heels? Scratch the manager's car with your house key? Or call back and plead for a second chance?

Hopefully not. Taking "no" as a personal rejection won't help your job-search effort. If you don't get the offer, you can still gain from the experience in two ways. First get the hiring manager's advice on what, if anything, you might do in the next interview to improve your presentation. If you're making serious mistakes, you'll want to correct them, not keep making them.

Simply call the manager, and communicate that although you were disappointed in not getting the job you still believe he or she made a good decision. Tell the manager you would appreciate any suggestions or advice he or she may have to help you interview for future positions. Listen to what the manager says. Don't debate the person's perceptions, simply try to understand and learn from them.

Second, you can learn from a rejection by approaching the hiring manager as a source of referrals and job leads. If you were one of the finalists for the position, the manager recognized your value and wished he or she had more than one position available. If this is the case, then give this person another chance to be an advocate for you by referring you to other interested hiring managers.

This type of follow-up will not only help further your job search; it will also position you positively in the mind of the hiring manager. You'll be remembered as a learner, and an initiator. If the individual who WAS hired doesn't work out, or has to leave in a few months, you stand a better chance of being next in line.

Putting It All Together in Marketing

Now, you will see the difference an interview can make in landing the job. **Turn to page 61 and read through Marketing #9, "A Tale of Two Interviews."**

Welcome Back

Before you leave this section on job interviews and offers, there are several special areas you need to consider:

Remember references. Either prior to or after a job interview, you'll be asked to provide references to the employer. When you wonder who to ask for a reference, it's good to follow these guidelines:

1. Reference only individuals who you know will speak positively and highly of you.

2. Reference people who will have credibililty in the eyes of the employer. (Mom and Dad are out!)

3. Tell your references the strengths you would like them to emphasize.

4. If you left your past employer on bad terms, go back and try to reconcile your differences. You never know when you'll need his or her reference.

5. Avoid sending references that begin with, "To whom it may concern." The more personal you make your communication the better.

6. If you're asked to give three names, and open (you can read it) or closed (you can't) references, make sure the references are "closed" (in a sealed envelope, mark as confidential). It carries more weight than an "open" letter.

Lastly, consider this: Why not use a reference to get the interview? If you know someone who believes in you and would have credibility with the hiring manager, then ask him or her to give a call on your behalf. Here's how such a call might go:

"Ms. Smith, my name is Ellen Jones. I'm operations manager for CID, and former supervisor of Bill French, an applicant for the position of operations coordinator in your company. I don't want to take much of your time. My purpose in calling is simply to recommend Bill as an outstanding candidate for the position, and to offer myself as a reference when, and if, it's appropriate."

A brief conversation similar to the one above can go a long way in getting you an interview; additional PR doesn't hurt!

Remember, nonverbal communication speaks! Whatever you do in an interview, try to remember the most important nonverbal signals—body posture and good eye contact. Good posture communicates alertness and discipline. Eye contact communicates confidence, straightforwardness, concern, and warmth. You should use both during your interview.

Remember, there's always hope. If you were extremely nervous in the interview and didn't feel like yourself, if you're sure you blew it, don't panic. Call back the hiring manager. Explain that you didn't feel you represented yourself well in the interview. If there's an interest on the other end of the line, suggest that you'd appreciate the opportunity to meet briefly to further discuss the position.

To help you prepare for a job interview, here are 16 basic questions you should be prepared to answer:

1. Tell me about yourself.
2. What interests you most about the position?
3. What do you consider to be your major strengths?
4. Why are you leaving your current job?
5. What did you like best about your last job?
6. What motivates you?
7. What bothered you most about your last job?
8. What are you doing to improve yourself?
9. Where do you see yourself in five (ten) years?
10. What kind of contribution could you make to this organization?
11. How would you describe your strengths?
12. What are your weaknesses?
13. Why should I hire you?
14. With what kind of people do you work best?
15. How would you describe your ideal job?
16. What kind of money are you looking for?

Any potential employer who's seriously interested in hiring you will expect you to ask questions about the position you're pursuing. Some questions you might ask are:

1. What strengths do you see as essential for success in this position?
2. What needs do you see in the department/organization that should be addressed in this position?
3. What type of person would best fit into the department/organization?
4. Will there be any changes in the near future that would significantly affect this position?
5. What is the primary purpose of the position?
6. When was the last time the position was open?
7. Where do people who leave this position tend to go?
8. What type of supervision would a person in this position receive?
9. What do you most appreciate about the department/organization?
10. What would you like to see changed in the department/organization?

Word of Encouragement. Hopefully, you're not overwhelmed by all the steps involved in marketing yourself. Our purpose has been to equip you with the tools and strategies essential for completing one of life's hardest tasks—looking for a job. In this effort, the pay is low, and the work is hard. However, the rewards can be outstanding. The effort you expend in packaging, promoting, and placing yourself in front of hiring managers will pay off. As you actively wait to see what God has for you. As you think positively about your strengths, and request assistance. And as you carry out the relevant action discussed in this marketing section! When you commit yourself to these tasks, you're exercising wise stewardship in career-decision making. Remember, you don't walk alone. You can walk confidently and responsibly with the Lord through this challenging life-task.

In this final section of the chapter you'll learn how to prepare for the trip, keep on the road, and fight the possible discouragements that can accompany your journey to the next job.

MAKING IT HAPPEN!

The best information, insight, strategies, and methods in the world are of little value unless you apply them. And in Career Kit we want to equip you to do your part to discover God's best for your worklife.

This discovery process takes both a practical and mystical form when applied to your job search. The practical side involves the specific tasks and activities that you're responsible for in your job search. As we've mentioned, finding your place in the workworld is a process of stewardship. There are risks and responsibilities that only you can take.

However, there is also a mystical side to this adventure. That's best summed up in Ecclesiastes 9:11:

"... the race is not to the swift or the battle to the strong nor does food come to the wise or wealth to the brilliant or favor to the learned; but time and chance happen to them all."

How to be Realistic During Your Job Search

While you pursue practical, relevant action in looking for work, you're also looking for and believing in those "breaks," and "opportunities" that cannot be predicted or prescribed, but that play an important part in your future success.

Life is both what you see, and what you can't see. It's part logical and illogical, planned and unpredictable, safe and scary, full of hope and, at times, marked by despair. Your search for work is a part of life. Expect it to encompass all of the above. Pursue the practical and "do-able." Yet, look for and expect the illogical and unpredictable. Realize that both responsibility and time will play a vital role in your search. Avoid the trap of developing a convenient loyalty to one over the other.

To help you move forward on both fronts, we've outlined specific steps you can take to conduct your job search in a way that will both cause you to look at life realistically and yet will invite you to exercise faith.

1. Get organized

Looking for work is a job. It requires specific tools and demands specific tasks. The first step in doing the job is becoming organized. The tools you'll need include:

• Appointment book — pocket-size with spaces for hourly appointments.

• Notepad/folder—preferably full-size (8 1/2 x 11") with spaces for carrying resume copies. Use it for taking notes during R&R interviews or recalling questions to ask during a job interview. Be sure it looks good! No ripped covers, taped sides, etc.

• Matching stationery—should have plain paper and envelopes to match your resume. Plain paper can be used for cover letters and thank-you notes.

• 3 x 5 cards and file box—at least 50 to 100 cards to write down and track referrals, and their sources. Remember, these contacts should be saved for future reference.

• Stamps—depending on the strategies you use, 50 to 100 stamps.

• Miscellaneous supplies—paper clips, staples, tape, file folders, etc. These are basic but essential.

• Phone-answering machine — Most of your time is going to be spent out in the marketplace, not at home. You need some way to catch incoming calls. A phone answering machine is the answer. You can rent or buy one. Or, ask a friend or relative who's home most hours and willing to take messages, or ask your current (discreet!) secretary if you have one. Don't overlook this important strategy; most employers won't call you twice.

• Quality copying service—you should have copies of all correspondence, cover letters, resumes, applications, etc. Find a printing shop, graphics firm, or copy center. You might even set up an account to spread out the costs if you're unemployed.

• Consistent typing/word processing support—looking for work involves formal communication. You need consistent, easy access to a reliable typist with a quality machine. Unless you meet these qualifications, don't type your own correspondence, because you'll be penny wise and pound foolish. Even if you have to pay someone, make sure your typing is done well. No erasures, typos or wrong formats.

• Specific work area—you need a place to write, think, make calls and track your progress. If you're unemployed, then explore possibilities outside of your home (vacant office space in church or business of a friend). You might even set up a "flexible shop" in a study room at the library. Make it a formal work space, a place where you can concentrate on getting the job done.

2. Set realistic expectations.

Don't set yourself up for failure and disappointment. Be realistic in considering what it takes to make a job/career change. Here are some principles to guide your expectations.

• As a rule of thumb, expect to spend at least one month of intensive job search for every $10,000 of income you expect on your next job.

• If you're making a major career change, then expect to spend three to six months actively searching for employment.

• If you're currently employed, double the time involved in looking for a new job.

SWING AWAY!
NEVER LET THE FEAR OF STRIKING OUT GET IN YOUR WAY.
BABE RUTH

• Remember, one out of every 25 R&R interviews turns up a job interview. That means 24 "nos" before you get a "yes!" Expect this.

Write out 24 "nos" followed by one "yes." Every time you conduct an R&R interview with no resulting job interview or lead, cross out a no, and then remember you're that much closer to a "yes."

• Expect to keep looking for a job until you have accepted a position. Don't start putting your eggs in one basket just because a great opportunity pops up. Wanting a job badly doesn't mean you'll get it. If you stop your search in hopes of one job, and you don't get the offer, recovering from the emotional letdown is twice as hard.

3. Expect to pay the price.

Like most jobs, the task of looking for work has its expenses. Here are some basic items you need to consider:

Basic wardrobe update	$250-400
Resume preparation and stationery	30-75
Office supplies	15-25
Copying costs	30-50
Stamps	10-20
Typing assistance	0-100
Phone answering machine	0-150
Gas and parking	30-100
Meals with networking contacts	0-150
Total	$235-1070

Looking for work is not the time to cut costs. Invest the money you feel is necessary to find the right job. If you increase your income by ten percent on your next job, or cut down the job search by one month (realistic results if you do your part), then you'll have more than recovered your initial investment.

4. Initiate relevation action.

Success in your job search depends upon initiating specific relevant activity. Here's a timetable to follow:

DEADLINE	GOAL
1st Week	Develop an appropriate resume to open doors or to remind employers of your potential.
1st Week	Identify 50 top contacts you'll either phone or write for suggestions and/or referrals.
1st Week	Generate a list of 10-20 promotional statements to communicate your strengths. Commit these to memory.
2nd-3rd Week	Through referrals or direct source contacts, get the names and titles of at least 50 hiring managers to contact (100 is preferred).
3rd-7th Week	Set up a minimum of eight referrals/interviews per week. Avoid Monday mornings, Friday afternoons, schedule no more than two per day.
2nd-7th Week	Identify two other strategies for generating job leads. (Visit organizations, call hotlines, read publications, etc.) Set aside a specific day of the week for pursuing these. Write thank-you notes the same day as R&R or job interviews.
7th week-ongoing	Develop another list of 50 contacts for advice and job leads.
7th week ongoing	Recontact past referrals to let them know you're still looking for work. Ask them for any more leads they may have.
7th week ongoing	If necessary, consider alternative, temporary, or part-time employment options.
7th week-ongoing	If you have received minimal interviews or offers, take time to reassess: job, target, appearance, promotional strength of your materials, and/or interview performance. Talk with friends/employers you trust; seek suggestions from a reliable career counselor.

1. Make a point to spend daily time praying and reading the Bible. Reflect on scripture passages that best relate to your situation. These might include: Jeremiah 29:11; Matthew 7:7; 2 Timothy 2:12; 2 Corinthians 4:16-17; Philippians 1:6. What other verses come to mind?

2. Follow up on every lead. This is a tremendous way to exercise your faith. Covenant, at the beginning of your job search, to take every referral, suggestion, or job lead seriously. By doing so, you give God the opportunity to direct you through whomever He may choose. You also relinquish ultimate control to Him and exercise obedience in seeking direction.

3. Allow others in the church body to minister to you. Looking for work is not a task you should attempt alone. As a Christian, you need others to pray for you, and encourage you. You need trusted friends to confirm and/or question your thinking, and to listen to your frustrations.

Seek out a support group at a church and meet regularly. Ask a few friends who can hold you accountable and encourage you. Ask one or two people who know you well to provide a listening ear and wise counsel as job opportunities and questions come up. Whatever you do, don't try to go it all alone.

How to Exercise Faith During Your Job Search

Looking for a job can be hard work, mentally and physically. And it can also be a spiritual challenge. During a job search, you're challenged to believe in your unique strengths and their value. You're challenged to take action and believe that the Lord will guide and direct your efforts. You're challenged to persist, even when there seems to be no visible solution or potential on the horizon. Faced with these challenges, how do you seek work and still have faith that things will eventually work out? Here are a few suggestions:

SUMMARY

In completing this chapter, you've moved into an ever-growing minority of job seekers who are properly equipped to find the right job. No longer will you play the "waiting game" in seeking employment. Now that you understand marketing, you know the specific steps needed to search for work. With prayer, preparation, and perseverance, you can take an active role in finding better employment, realizing that the Lord is going before you and beside you all the way. You now know how to find a balance between exercising responsibility and finding work.

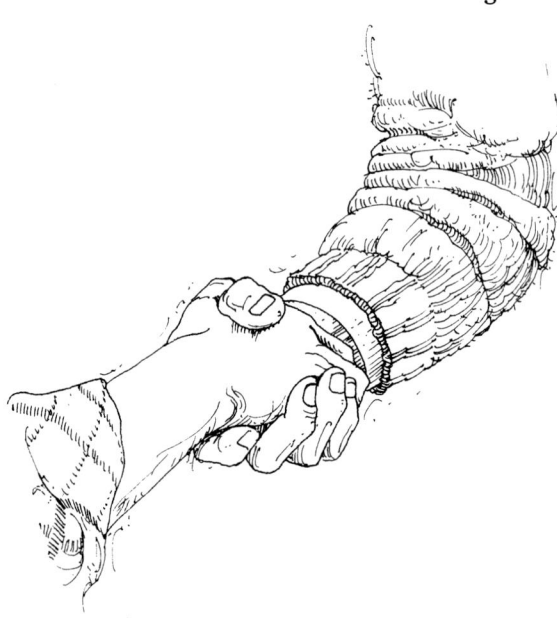

In addition, you have fine-tuned skills that have been used in previous job searches. The new insight you've gained regarding how to identify job openings, prepare resumes, and interview will enhance and accelerate your next job search. The perspective you learned on promotion will enable you to speak confidently but accurately about yourself to potential employers. Knowing realistically how much time and energy is involved in finding the right job will help you avoid the discouragement that comes from unrealistic expectations in your job search.

When you purchased Career Kit, you were probably feeling the "winds of change" blowing through your life. In completing chapters one through four, you may have sorted out why you were considering a career change. However, it is entirely possible that getting God's perspective, assessing yourself, exploring your options, and marketing yourself have not clarified whether or not you should make a change. The reason is that many other factors contribute to this desire for change. Some are legitimate reasons and some are not. How can you know if a change in your worklife is in order?

After success at the Inn, Jacob reached this point of creative tension in his own career. He had a difficult but necessary choice to make: to stay at the Inn or pursue his stained glass work full time. The "winds of change" were blowing through his worklife and demanding his attention. It was time for Jacob to conduct a checkup and take appropriate action.

Maybe it's time for you to conduct a checkup and, like Jacob, objectively evaluate a change in your worklife. Chapter Five, the final chapter in Career Kit, will guide you through this important and final step in Career decision-making.

Bibliography

Alessandra, Anthony J. *Non-Manipulative Selling.* Reston, Virginia. Reston Publishing Company, Inc. A Prentice-Hall Company, 1979.

Allen, Jeffrey G. *How to Turn an Interview into a Job.* New York. Simon & Schuster, 1983.

Baehler, James R. *Book of Perks.* New York. Rinehart and Winston, 1983.

Bixler, Susan. *The Professional Image.* New York. G.P. Putnam's Sons, 1984.

Cohen, William A. *The Executive's Guide to Finding a Superior Job.* New York, 1978.

Djeddah, Eli. *Moving Up.* Berkeley, California. Ten Speed Press, 1978.

Douglas, Martha C. *Go For It!* Berkeley, California. Ten Speed Press, 1983.

Greco, Benedetto. *How to Get the Job That's Right for You.* Homewood, Illinois. Dow Jones Irwin, 1980.

Haldane, Bernard, Jean Haldane and Lowell Martin. *Job Power.* Washington, D.C. Acropolis Books Ltd, 1980.

Half, Robert. *The Robert Half Way to Get Hired in Today's Job Market.* New York. Bantam Books, 1983.

Jackson, Tom. *Guerrilla Tactics in the Job Market.* New York. Bantam Books, Inc. 1978.

Jackson, Tom. *The Perfect Resume.* Garden City, New York. Anchor Press/Doubleday, 1981.

Jeffers, William R. *Selling Yourself (The Way to a Better Job).* Englewood Cliffs, New Jersey. Prentice Hall, Inc., 1979.

Lathrop, Richard. *Who's Hiring Who.* Berkeley, California. Ten Speed Press, 1977.

Marcon, Mike, and Margot Worthington. *Twelve Steps to Finding a Job Under $30,000 in Four Weeks.* Englewood Cliffs, New Jersey. Prentice Hall, Inc. 1984.

Medley, Anthony. *Sweaty Palms, The Neglected Art of Being Interviewed.* Belmont, California. Lifetime Learning Publications, a division of Wadsworth Publishing Company, Inc., 1978.

Merman, Stephen K. and John E. McLaughlin. *Out-Interviewing the Interviewer.* Englewood Cliffs, New Jersey. Prentice-Hall, Inc., 1983.

Molloy, John T. *Dress for Success.* New York. Warner Books, 1975.

Molloy, John T. *The Woman's Dress For Success Book.* New York. Warner Books, 1977.

Rogers, Edward J. *Getting Hired.* Englewood Cliffs, New Jersey. Prentice-Hall Inc., 1982.

Rosaluk, Warren J. *Throw Away Your Resume and Get That Job!* Englewood Cliffs, New Jersey. Prentice-Hall Inc., 1983.

Sheard, James L., Rodney E. Stalley, and David L. Williamson. *Opening Doors to the Job Market.* Minneapolis, Minnesota. Augsburg Publishing House, 1983.

EXERCISES

MARKETING #1: Focusing on Your Features

The goal of this exercise is to identify the features you possess that would be appealing to a hiring manager considering you for the job you are pursuing.

Suggested time: 30 minutes

Instructions

1. Fill in your job objective in the space provided.
2. Identify from your background any education/training, work experience, responsibilities, or character qualities you possess that are related to your job objective. Write these features below in the far right column.
3. Summarize your five most important features in the space provided.
4. Return to page 14, Chapter Four and continue.

1. My Job Objective is:

2. Attractive features I possess relative to this objective:

CATEGORY	EXAMPLES	MY FEATURES
Education/Training	Bachelors Degree in Communication, or A.A. Degree in Food Service Management	
Work Experience	Five years Customer Service for Blue Cross, or As a volunteer, have co-ordinated 20 picnics for office.	
Responsibilities	Supervised eight employees Managed Budget Operated Computer Terminal	
Character Qualities	Diplomatic Curious Enthusiastic Diligent	

3. In Reference to my objective the five most appealing features I possess are:

1.

2.

3.

4.

5.

MARKETING #2: Building Your Benefits

The goal of this exercise is to translate your five most appealing features from Marketing #1 into benefits you can express and support to a potential employer.

Suggested Time: 30 minutes

Instructions
1. Read through the examples of how to translate features into benefits that you can support from experience.
2. Using the top five features identified in Marketing #1, translate them into employee benefits, and then support your claims with evidence from your experience.
3. Return to page 14, Chapter Four and continue.

1. Examples:

Seeking position as Feature Employer Benefit Support	Nurse Interpersonal Communication Increased patient cooperation Was asked to speak with belligerent patient who was refusing medication and disrupting the floor. After a 20-minute conversation patient vented frustration, fears, proceeded to take medication and cooperated with surgical preorientation.
Seeking position as Feature Employer benefits Support	Account representative Selling Increased revenue As paid sales representative, was challenged with the least productive account list. Within six months, generated 60% of station's total sales.
Seeking position as Feature Employer benefit Support	Bookkeeper Streamlining procedures Improved service/reduction in errors Suggested several changes in payroll system that eliminated errors by 30% and enabled checks to be distributed two days earlier.

2. Feature #1:

   Benefit:

   Support:

Feature #2:
Benefit:
Support:

Feature #3:
Benefit:
Support:

Feature #4:
Benefit:
Support:

Feature #5:
Benefit:
Support:

3. Return to page 14, Chapter Four.

MARKETING #3: Affirming your Advantages

The goal of this exercise is to remember and affirm the distinctives you possess that can be assets in your job search.

Suggested time: 20 minutes

Instructions

1. In light of your job objective, consider your age, experience, training, geographic location, looks, sex, ethnic background, size, current employment situation, financial condition, marital status, design, people-connections, etc.—any distinctive you possess that has implications for your job search.

2. In the spaces below, list those distinctives and address the positive aspects of each one. Try to come up with ten.

3. Return to page 15, Chapter Four and continue.

	Distinctive	**Advantage**
1.		
2.		
3.		
4.		
5		
6.		
7.		
8.		
9.		
10.		

MARKETING #4: Networking to Identify Hiring Managers

The goal of this exercise is to equip you to initiate communication with your contacts in order to identify hiring managers.

Suggested time: 30 minutes

Instructions

1. Read through the sample phone conversation.
2. Write out a phone script you will use to solicit the help of your contacts.
3. Write out a phone script you will use to follow up the leads you receive from your contacts.
4. Return to page 26, Chapter Four.

---

1. Sample Networking Conversation

Situation: Bill calls an old friend, Jim, who works in a large company that Bill is interested in.

Receptionist: "Ajax Corporation, this is Karen."

Bill: "Good morning, Karen, my name is Bill Smith. I'm calling to speak with Jim Marshall in accounting. Could you connect me please?"

Receptionist: "One moment, please."

RING-RING-RING—-

Jim's Secretary: "Accounting, Mr. Marshall's office. Can I help you?"

Bill: Yes. My name is Bill Smith, and I am calling to speak with Jim Marshall. Could you connect me please?"

Jim's Secretary: "Mr. Marshall is in a meeting right now, Mr. Smith. Maybe I could help you?"

Bill: "Thank you, but I really need to speak with Jim. Is there a better time to call?"

Jim's Secretary: "You might call back at 11:15."

Bill: "Thank you, I'll do that."

At 11:15 Bill dials directly to Jim's office.

RING-RING-RING—

Jim's Secretary: "Good morning, Accounting. Mr. Marshall's office."

Bill: "Good morning, this is Bill Smith calling again for Jim Marshall. Is Jim available?"

Secretary: "Yes, Mr. Smith. One moment, and I'll connect you."

Jim: "This is Marshall."

Bill: "Good morning, Jim, this is Bill Smith."

Jim: "Bill! How are you? I don't think we've talked since the high school reunion!"

Bill: "You're right, that's the last time we were together. It's been a while."

Jim: "I'll say. What's up?"

Bill: "Well, do you have a few minutes to talk?"

Jim: "I've got 'til 11:30."

Bill: "That's plenty of time. Let me explain my reason for calling. Since we last talked, I've decided to make a career change. I'm pursuing a position in purchasing. I thought you might be able to direct me in my job search."

Jim: "Bill, I'll help if I can. What kind of direction do you need?"

Bill: "Ajax Corporation is one of the companies I have targeted to explore employment possibilities. I would like to meet briefly with the purchasing manager at Ajax, introduce myself, share my background and strengths, and get his or her suggestions for my job search. I thought you might be able to refer me to this person at Ajax."

Jim: "Bill, I'm not sure who that would be. But I can give you the name of someone who would know."

Bill: "That would be great!"

Jim: "Call Carl Ward at extension 7394. Carl is Director of Administrative Services. He could tell you who to talk with."

Bill: "That's Carl Ward, extension 7394."

Jim: "Right."

Bill: "Would it be OK to tell Carl you referred me to him?"

Jim: "Oh sure!"

Bill: "Well, thanks Jim, you've been a great help. Let's get together before the next reunion comes around."

Jim: "Let's do it. Give me a call in a month and we'll set something up."

Bill: "Good idea. I'll do that. Thanks again, Jim."

Jim: "You're welcome. And good luck in your job search."

Bill calls Carl Ward:

RING-RING-RING—

Carl's Secretary: "Administrative Services, Mr. Ward's office."

Bill: "Good afternoon, my name is Bill Smith. I'm calling for Carl Ward. Could you connect me please?"

Secretary: "What is the nature of your call?"

Bill: "I was referred to Mr. Ward by Jim Marshall in accounting."

Secretary: "One moment please."

Carl: "This is Carl Ward."

Bill: "Mr. Ward, my name is Bill Smith. Jim Marshall in accounting suggested I give you a call. Do you have a minute to talk?"

Carl: "Yes, Bill. What can I do for you?"

Bill: "I'd like to speak briefly with the purchasing manager at Ajax. Jim Marshall thought you could direct me to this person."

Carl: "The person you want to talk with is Marge James. Marge is Central Services Manager. She is in charge of all our purchasing."

Bill: "So that would be Marge James. J A M E S?"

Carl: "Yes that's correct."

Bill: "And her title is Central Services Manager?"

Carl: "Correct."

Bill: "I won't take any more of your time Mr. Ward. Thank you for the information."

Carl: "You're welcome. Goodbye."

2. My phone script for networking with my contacts will be:

    Reminder: Keep your phone scripts direct and to the point. Work at using them without sounding stilted or apologetic. You have every right to initiate this type of communication. You are helping both yourself and the hiring manager.

    4. Return to page 26, Chapter Four.

3. My phone script for initiating contact with individuals I am referred to will be:

MARKETING #5: Identifying Hiring Managers Through Direct Contact

The goal of this exercise is to demonstrate how to contact organizations directly and identify the appropriate hiring manager.

Suggested time: 20 minutes

Instructions:

1. Read through the sample phone conversations.

2. Write out a phone script to use in initiating contact with the organization.

3. Return to page 26, Chapter Four.

---

1. Sample Conversation:

Situation: Jill wants to work as a financial aid counselor at a university. She has a list of universities in the state to contact.

RING-RING-RING—

Receptionist: "Coed University. Can I help you?"

Jill: "Yes, my name is Jill Matthews. I have some business information to send to the Director of Financial Aid at Coed. Could you give me his or her name and title so I can address this information appropriately?"

Receptionist: "One moment please... That would be Harold K. Rutsome. The last name is spelled R U T S O M E. His title is Financial Aid Director."

Jill: "That's Harold K. Rutsome. R U T S O M E. Financial Aid Director?"

Receptionist: "Correct."

Jill: "And the address I should use would be?"

Receptionist: "Coed University. PO Box 44372, Anywhere, U.S.A. 77349."

Jill: "That's Coed University, PO Box 44372, Anywhere, U.S.A. 77349."

Receptionist: "Right."

Jill: "Thank you for the information."

Receptionist: "You're welcome."

This sample script will, in most cases, enable you to identify the hiring manager quite easily.

2. My phone script for initiating contact with the organization will be:

MARKETING #6: Contacting Hiring Managers by Phone

The goal of this exercise is to equip you to confidently initiate phone contact with a potential hiring manager for the purpose of scheduling a referral interview.

Suggested time: 30 minutes
Instructions:

1. Read through the sample phone conversation.

2. Write out a phone script to use in your phone call.

3. Tape this phone script and listen to it. How do you sound? Are you confident? Is your voice natural or do you sound like you are reading a script? Practice your initial script until it becomes second nature to you. Call a friend and role play it if necessary.

4. Return to page 26, Chapter Four.

---

1. Sample telephone conversation:
   Situation: John has a background in accounting. He has targeted 50 companies he would like to work with. He has identified the hiring manager for each company. Now John must contact the hiring manager to schedule a referral interview.
RING-RING-RING—

H.M. Secretary: "Accounting, Ms. Tory's office."

John: "Good afternoon, this is John Emery, and I'm calling to speak with Janis Tory."

H.M. Secretary: "One moment, Mr. Emery."

Ms. Tory: "This is Janis Tory."

John: "Ms. Tory, my name is John Emery. I am an accountant and am pursuing a job change. Your company is very interesting to me. Realizing you may have a future need for my strengths, I would appreciate the opportunity to meet briefly with you, share my background, and receive any advice you may have for me as I pursue a new position. Would it be possible to schedule a 30-minute appointment with you next Tuesday morning?"

Ms. Tory: "I'm sorry Mr. Emery, but we have no positions open at this time."

John: "That's fine. I realize it's unlikely you would have an immediate need for my strengths. However, any direction or advice you could provide would be appreciated. Could we schedule a brief appointment?"

Ms. Tory: "To be honest, I'm really busy next week."

John: "I understand. When would there be a more convenient time for us to meet?"

Ms. Tory: "Well, let's see. Two weeks from today, I have some time in the morning. Early."

John: "That's the 23rd. I could meet that day any time before 10:00."

Ms. Tory: "How about 8:30?"

John: "8:30 would be fine, Ms. Tory."

Ms. Tory: "I'll put you down for a half-hour on the 23rd at 8:30."

John: "Great! Thank you for seeing me. I'll look forward to talking with you on the 23rd."

Ms. Tory: "You're welcome, John. Goodbye."

John: "Goodbye."

Did you notice:
- John was direct, to the point, without being pushy. He did not ask for work, but neither did he hide the fact that he would be interested in working for Ms. Tory.
- John did not get discouraged at the first sign of resistance in getting together with Ms. Tory. He moved her beyond the idea of not meeting because she didn't have an immediate opening. He did not let the fact that she was busy hinder his meeting with Ms. Tory.
- Without being demanding, John diplomatically pursued his goal of getting the opportunity to meet Ms. Tory face to face, giving her a chance to look him over, and gaining her advice for his job search.
- John did it, and so can YOU!

Here are two alternative phone scripts to use in contacting the hiring manager (H.M.)
Alternative #1

Hiring Manager: "This is Swartz."

Job Seeker: "Good morning, Mr. Swartz. My name is Jan Matthews. I'm calling to seek your professional advice. As a para legal, pursuing a job change, I would like to meet briefly with you, for 30 minutes— no longer. I'm not expecting you to have a job for me, but would appreciate any direction you could give in my job search. Could we schedule a time to meet this week?"

Alternative #2

Hiring Manager: "Marketing, this is Margaret Hansen."

Job Seeker: "Ms. Hansen, my name is Perry Rand. I followed your recent Marketing Campaign for General Services and was impressed with the approach. I have a strong marketing background and experience in the direction you are headed. Without being presumptuous, it's quite possible you may have a future need for the expertise I possess. My purpose in calling is to schedule an appointment with you to further explore your needs and my strengths. Could I buy you a lunch next Tuesday?"

2. The telephone script I will use in contacting a hiring manager is:

3. Practice this phone script.
4. Return to page 26, Chapter Four.

MARKETING #7: Contacting the Hiring Manager by Letter

The goal of this exercise is to demonstrate how to initiate contact with a hiring manager by letter.
Suggested time: 45 minutes
Note: The introductory letter is an effective way of contacting the hiring manager to set up a referral interview. Your letter stands an 80% chance of being read.

A good introductory letter will include the following:
- Personal introductory statement
- Identification of referral source (if you were referred)
- Brief statement of your situation
- Specific statement about what you want
- Follow-up statement
- Reference to an enclosed resume
- Statement about future contact
- Warm closing

The introductory letter should be brief and to the point. There is no reason to explain your situation in great detail.

Instructions:
1. Read through the sample letters.
2. Write out an introductory letter you can use to set up referral interviews.
3. Read through the follow-up telephone scripts.
4. Practice your phone skills with a friend. Role-play each of the situations.
5. Return to page 27 of Career Kit and continue.

Sample Introductory letter—With a Referral

June 6, 1985

Mr. J.D. Owens
Director of Food Service
Allen Senior Community
Seattle, WA 98119

Dear Mr. Owens,

I am writing at the suggestion of Don Green in Administrative Services. Mr. Green suggested it might be beneficial for the two of us to meet. Let me explain.

After six years in conference food service management, I am redirecting my career into a more stable setting. Past volunteer work with senior citizens has been so rewarding that I have decided to pursue serving this population professionally.

Acquainted with the fine reputation of Allen Senior Community, I would be very interested in exploring work possibilities with you. However, realizing you may have no immediate need for my strengths, any direction or advice you could provide at this time would be appreciated.

I would like to schedule a brief appointment with you to share my background and receive any suggestions you may have for my job search. The enclosed resume may be of help to you in advising me.

To that end, I'll telephone you within the week to schedule a mutually convenient appointment. Thank you for your time and consideration.

Sincerely,

Robert Lance
Robert Lance

Enclosure

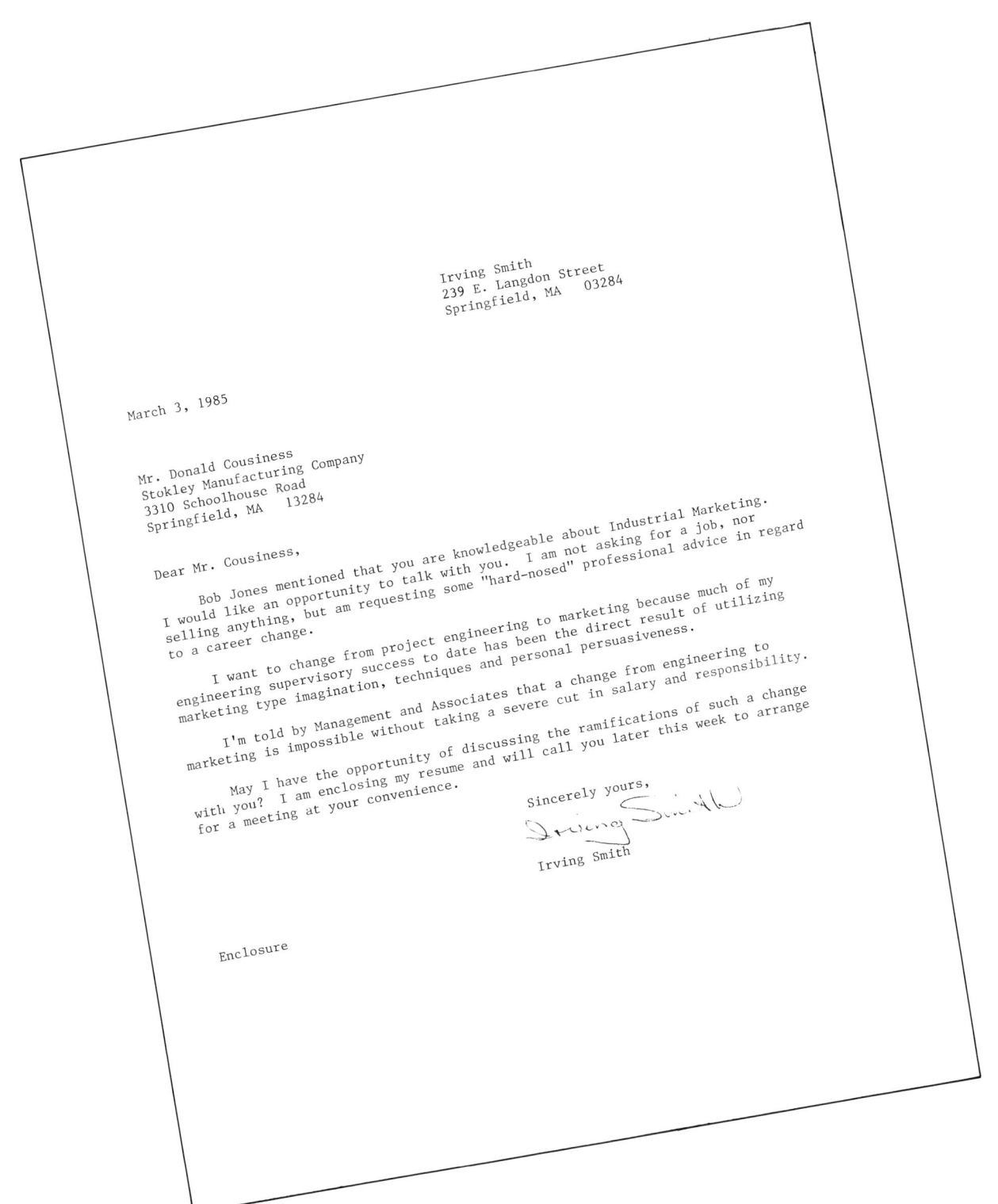

Sample Introductory letter—With a Referral

Irving Smith
239 E. Langdon Street
Springfield, MA   03284

March 3, 1985

Mr. Donald Cousiness
Stokley Manufacturing Company
3310 Schoolhouse Road
Springfield, MA   13284

Dear Mr. Cousiness,

    Bob Jones mentioned that you are knowledgeable about Industrial Marketing. I would like an opportunity to talk with you. I am not asking for a job, nor selling anything, but am requesting some "hard-nosed" professional advice in regard to a career change.

    I want to change from project engineering to marketing because much of my engineering supervisory success to date has been the direct result of utilizing marketing type imagination, techniques and personal persuasiveness.

    I'm told by Management and Associates that a change from engineering to marketing is impossible without taking a severe cut in salary and responsibility.

    May I have the opportunity of discussing the ramifications of such a change with you? I am enclosing my resume and will call you later this week to arrange for a meeting at your convenience.

Sincerely yours,

Irving Smith

Enclosure

Sample Introductory letter—Without a Referral

March 8, 1985

Mr. Gary Strong
Controller
Western Drive
3300 West Ansley Street
St. Louis, MO 52783

Dear Mr. Strong,

    I am writing to seek your professional advice. After a brief leave of absence to complete a Master's Degree in Business Administration, I am re-entering the accounting field. A growing interest in cost accounting has led me to pursue employment in the manufacturing industry.

    Realizing you may have a future need for someone with my background, I would appreciate the opportunity to meet briefly with you (30 minutes, no longer!) to share my strengths as well as receive any advice you may have for my job search. The enclosed resume may assist you in advising me.

    I will telephone you this Thursday to schedule a mutually convenient appointment.

Thank you for your time and consideration.

Respectfully,

Scott Pool

Scott Pool

Enclosure

Sample Introductory letter—Without a Referral

November 30, 1984

William D. Christiansen
Vice President for Operations
C.D.C. Inc.
Harrison, IA 78632

Dear Mr. Christiansen,

At 55, with 15 years experience as Chief Operations Officer, continuing to learn and produce on the job is more important to me than any previous or future job title.

A recent merger has eliminated the position I held for the past ten years. Although capable of an early retirement, my career in operations has been so rewarding that I would like to extend it as much as possible. I'm writing to you to seek your assistance in doing so.

The enclosed resume highlights my contributions and work history. My goal is to use this background in whatever capacity would be most useful to a company.

To that end, I would like to meet briefly with you to gain your suggestions and advice on how I can best achieve this goal. May I telephone you next Tuesday to schedule an appointment?

Thanks for your time and consideration.

Sincerely,

Richard Leary
Richard Leary

Enclosure

2. My introductory letter to set up a referral letter will read as follows:

3. Read through these telephone scripts for follow-up calls to the introductory letter.

Situation: The hiring manager misunderstands your intention. She or he thinks you are asking for a job.

RING-RING-RING—

H.M. Secretary: "Daily Ministries, Ms. Scott's office."

Job Seeker: "Yes, this is Jim Thornton calling for Ms. Scott.

Secretary: "One moment please."

Ms. Scott: "This is Gloria Scott, can I help you?"

Jim: "Ms. Scott, my name is Jim Thornton. I'm calling to follow up the letter and resume I sent you last week. Did you receive my information?"

Ms. Scott: "Yes Jim, I have. I've forwarded the information to personnel. I suggest you contact them about possibilities."

Jim: "I appreciate your help Ms. Scott. As mentioned in my letter, I didn't expect you to have a job for me. However I would like to meet briefly with you, get your insights into the industry and receive any direction or advice you may have for my job search. Could we schedule an appointment next week?"

Ms. Scott: "Let me look at my calendar . . ."

Situation: The hiring manager has not received the information you sent.

RING-RING-RING—

H.M. Secretary: "Daily Ministries, Ms. Scott's office."

Job Seeker: "This is Jim Thornton, I'm calling for Ms. Scott."

Secretary: "May I tell Ms. Scott why you are calling?"

Jim: "Yes, I'm following up the information I sent to Ms. Scott last week."

Secretary: "One moment please."

Ms. Scott: "This is Gloria Scott."

Jim: "Good morning Ms. Scott. My name is Jim Thornton. I'm calling to follow up the resume and letter I sent you last week. Have you had an opportunity to review them?"

Ms. Scott: "I'm sorry Jim, I have not received any information from you. But I can tell you we have no openings."

Jim: "That's fine—although I am seeking employment in public relations, I realized it is unlikely you would have an immediate need for my strengths. My purpose in writing was to meet briefly with you to discuss my background and receive any advice or suggestions you may have for my job search. Could we schedule a 30-minute appointment for next Wednesday?"

Ms. Scott: "Quite honestly Jim, I'm extremely busy and just don't have the time right now."

Jim: "I understand. Would there be someone else at Daily who might advise me?"

Ms. Scott: "I suppose you could talk with my assistant director."

Jim: "Good idea. I would be interested in doing that . . ."

Ms. Scott: "Well, his name is Fred Hansen. Fred's extension is 362."

Jim: "When I contact Mr. Hansen, can I tell him you suggested we meet briefly?"

Ms. Scott: "Yes, in fact, I'll tell Fred to expect a call from you."

Jim: "That's very generous. Ms. Scott, thank you for your assistance. You have been very helpful."

Ms. Scott: "You're welcome Jim. Goodbye."

Jim: "Goodbye."

Situation: The hiring manager has received the information and is expecting the call.

RING-RING-RING—

H.M. Secretary: "Daily Ministries, Ms. Scott's office."

Job Seeker: "This is Jim Thornton, I'm calling for Ms. Scott."

Secretary: "One moment Mr. Thornton."

Ms. Scott: "This is Gloria Scott."

Jim: "Ms. Scott. My name is Jim Thornton, and I'm calling to follow up the resume and cover letter I sent to you last week. Have you received the information and had a chance to review it?"

Ms. Scott: "Yes, I have Jim."

Jim: "Great! As I mentioned in my letter, I would like to schedule a brief appointment with you. Could we get together next Tuesday afternoon?"

Ms. Scott: "Tuesday is fine, Jim. How about 2:30?"

Jim: "2:30 is fine for me."

Ms. Scott: "Well, I'll see you then."

Jim: "Thank you Ms. Scott. I'll look forward to talking with you. Goodbye."

4.. Practice your phone skills with a friend.

5. Return to page 27, Chapter Four.

MARKETING #8: Conducting a Referral Interview

The goal of this exercise is to give you an example of how to approach a referral interview.

Suggested time: 10 minutes

Instructions:

1. Read through the sample interview. Notice the flow of the conversation.

Sample Referral Interview

Job Seeker: "Mr. Jones, Good morning, I'm Art Lange. It's a pleasure to meet you."

Hiring Manager: "Thank you, please have a seat, Art."

Job Seeker: "I appreciate your taking the time to meet with me today."

Hiring Manager: "You're quite welcome. I'm always interested in talking to someone about purchasing."

Job Seeker: "I would appreciate any advice or assistance you could give to me. By the way, how did you get involved in purchasing?"

Hiring Manager: "Well, I started out as a corporate 'go-for' in the central services department, was asked to purchase chairs and desks for a new wing we were adding on, found I enjoyed scanning the marketplace for the best deals, and was good at negotiating with vendors. A purchasing department was opened a few years later, I applied for a position and was hired."

Job Seeker: "So you've stayed with the same company all these years?"

Hiring Manager: "Oh no, I have moved several times since then. I've purchased everything from car fleets to cattle feed. It's a fascinating field."

Job Seeker: "Sounds like you really enjoy your work?"

Hiring Manager: "I do!"

Job Seeker: "As I mentioned on the phone, I'm making a career change into purchasing. Like you, I have purchased several items in other jobs and really enjoyed it. I find that getting the best deal for a company is a real challenge. I was very successful at it. At this time, I'm looking for a job as a purchasing assistant. I've developed a resume highlighting my purchasing-related experience. Would you mind critiquing it for me?"

Hiring Manager: "Not at all. Let me take a look at it."

Job Seeker: (hands hiring manager resume—if not mailed in advance)

Hiring Manager: "Hmmm... so you saved your organization $2,000 on the purchase of a copier."

Job Seeker: "Yes, that was a real challenge. Especially to get a complete service contract with the reduced price."

Hiring Manager: "I agree, a good price isn't much of a deal if you end up paying an arm and a leg for service. You haven't mentioned a membership in the purchasing association; you HAVE joined?"

Job Seeker: "I was waiting to join after getting a purchasing position. Would you recommend I join now?"

Hiring Manager: "Definitely, it shows you're serious about pursuing the field. It's also a great source of job leads."

Job Seeker: "That's good advice, I'll follow up on that today."

Hiring Manager: "Have you taken any course work in purchasing? You know the field is getting more specialized each day."

Job Seeker: "That's what I've heard. I'm currently enrolled in a purchasing class at Coed Community College."

Hiring Manager: "Good, I would emphasize that in your resume."

Job Seeker: "Good point! Based upon my resume, do you see any difficulties in my pursuing a purchasing assistant position?"

Hiring Manager: "Not as long as you focus on office equipment types of purchasing."

Job Seeker: "So you would suggest I limit my job search to that particular area?"

Hiring Manager: "Yes. The field is so competitive, it's a waste of time to pursue a position unless you have some experience in it."

Job Seeker: "I see. Then you think my current experience is adequate for an office equipment purchasing position?"

Hiring Manager: "Yes, I would say so."

Job Seeker: "Are you aware of any organizations having current or future openings in this area of purchasing?"

Hiring Manager: "Not off hand."

Job Seeker: "Could you suggest any purchasing managers I might talk with to explore employment possibilities?"

Hiring Manager: "Well, you might give Jim Welch a call at Pyro Tech. They do a lot of office equipment work. I think I have his number here."

Job Seeker: "Is that Welch—W E L C H?"

Hiring Manager: "Right."

Job Seeker: "And his title is...?"

Hiring Manager: "Central Services Director. He's in charge of purchasing. His number is 777-5351."

Job Seeker: "Great! Would it be OK to use your name as a reference in contacting him?"

Hiring Manager: "Sure, no problem."

Job Seeker: "Anyone else who might help me in my job search?"

Hiring Manager: "No one comes to mind. Can I keep a copy of your resume? We may have some openings in the near future. You never know."

Job Seeker: "I would appreciate your keeping me in mind. Would you mind if I followed up with you by phone in two weeks to give you an update and get any additional suggestions you might have at that time?"

Hiring Manager: "That would be fine. I'm usually free Friday afternoons. Why don't you give me a call then."

Job Seeker: "Thanks, I'll do that. Could I get your advice on one more thing before I go?"

Hiring Manager: "That depends on what it is."

Job Seeker: "Do you have any suggestions on how I could improve the way I present myself?"

Hiring Manager: "I think you've come across very professionally. My only suggestion would be wear a more business-looking outfit. You meet and negotiate with a lot of vendors in purchasing. A 'business type' look is important."

Job Seeker: "Good point. You have been most helpful. Thank you for your time and suggestions."

Hiring Manager: "You're very welcome. Good luck in your job search."

2. Return to page 27 of Chapter Four.

MARKETING #9:
A Tale of Two Interviews

The goal of this exercise is to demonstrate the difference interviewing techniques can make.

Suggested time: 1 hour

Instructions:

1. Read through the sample interviews.

2. Note the differences between the two interviews in terms of:
- Developing an initial rapport with the hiring manager
- Identifying the hiring manager's needs and concerns
- Job seeker's response to sensitive questions (i.e. leaving last job, money, experience)
- Job seeker's ability to promote his or her strengths
- How the interview was ended

3. Consider your last job interview. How could you improve it? Check off areas to work on.

4. Practice these areas with a friend. Tape your responses and listen to them.

5. Return to page 37 of Chapter Four and continue.

---

1. Sample Interviews
Interview #1

Hiring Manager: "Good morning, Mr. Lake, come in and have a seat."

Job Seeker: "Thank you."

Hiring Manager: "So you're interested in the position as Lead Operator?"

Job Seeker: "Yes, I am."

Hiring Manager: "Have you had any experience as a lead?"

Job Seeker: "Well uh, not directly, but it sounds interesting and I'm sure I could learn it."

Hiring Manager: "I see; well tell me Mr. Lake, what interests you in our company?"

Job Seeker: "I've had several friends work here and they say it's a great place to work. I know the benefits are good, too."

Hiring Manager: "Yes, I guess that's true. I'm curious Mr. Lake. According to this resume, you stayed at your last job less than a year, it that right?"

Job Seeker: "Yes, that's right, I had to get out of that place."

Hiring Manager: "I see; what happened?"

Job Seeker: "Well, the boss and I just couldn't get along. He was the type of person that was never pleased with anybody. You know what I mean? He really wore on my nerves, so I decided to leave."

Hiring Manager: "That's too bad; so you're unemployed at the present?"

Job Seeker: "That's right. I'm really anxious to get back to work."

Hiring Manager: "What kind of money are you looking for?"

Job Seeker: "Well, money isn't that important to me at this point; it's really the right job that I'm looking for."

Hiring Manager: "Tell me, Mr. Lake, what are you looking for in a job?"

Job Seeker: "I'd like a boss who treats me fairly, good benefits and the opportunity to move up in the company."

Hiring Manager: "I see; well our time is about up. Do you have any questions about the position?"

Job Seeker: "Yes. When would I start if I was hired?"

Hiring Manager: "We hope to have someone in the position by the 15th of the month."

Job Seeker: "That would be great."

Hiring Manager: "Any other questions?"

Job Seeker: "No, that's all I guess."

Hiring Manager: "Well, it's been nice talking to you, Mr. Lake. You'll be hearing from us."

Job Seeker: "Thank you!"

Interview #2

Hiring Manager: "Good morning, Mr. Jones, come in and have a seat."

Job Seeker: "Thank you, Mr. Hall. This is a lovely office building; have you been here long?"

Hiring Manager: "Six years this spring. It is a nice place to work."

Job Seeker: "I noticed the tennis trophy on your credenza. Are you an avid player?"

Hiring Manager: "Yes, I play quite regularly; how about you?"

Job Seeker: "I enjoy the game a lot. I would like to play more than I do."

Hiring Manager: "I feel the same way. Well, so you're interested in the position as Lead Operator?"

Job Seeker: "Yes, I am, Mr. Hall. In studying the job description, my background and strengths seem to be well-suited for the job. But I was interested in knowing what your concerns are about the position? Or what particular strengths you see are needed at this time? What do you think?"

Hiring Manager: "Well, to be quite honest, I think we need someone with solid experience. I've had my fill of novices at this job."

Job Seeker: "It sounds like you've had problems hiring individuals with minimal experience."

Hiring Manager: "A lot of problems. It's reflecting bad on the department."

Job Seeker: "I see. What kind of problems are you experiencing?"

Hiring Manager: "Quotas aren't being met for one. The last two leads I had just haven't been able to get the production out. They just didn't know the job well enough."

Job Seeker: "Inexperience is no excuse for low productivity. In fact I've found on my last two jobs that although I came in with minimal experience, with a little homework and asking the right questions, I was exceeding quotas within a few weeks . . ."

Hiring Manager: "I see, well tell me, what do you know about the job?"

Job Seeker: "I know it requires a lot of detailed calculations. Math has always been a strong suit. I memorize formulas quickly and seem to be able to work through them faster than most. Another important strength is watching each step of the process closely. I have a strong eye for detail. My error ratio in my last job was less than 2%. Would you agree that these are critical requirements for the job?"

Hiring Manager: "Definitely. You can't be a good operator without a mind for math and a careful eye. Say, I noticed you left your last job after only one year, what happened?"

Job Seeker: "Well, I was very successful in my job. However, there was a change in management and the quantity and quality of production started to drop. I felt I was capable of making a greater contribution, and decided to seek a better opportunity."

Hiring Manager: "I see. What interests you in our company?"

Job Seeker: "I've talked with several competitors. You have an excellent reputation and are growing; that means increasing production efforts. I find it a challenge to increase production without cutting quality. Working as a lead operator seems to provide that kind of challenge."

Hiring Manager: "Tell me, Mr. Jones. What kind of money are you looking for?"

Job Seeker: "Money is important, and I'm sure you would be fair. I'm not that familiar with your particular company salary schedules. What is the range for this type of position?"

Hiring Manager: "This is a grade 22 position which starts at $1450/month and goes to $2200/month."

Job Seeker: "$2200/month is certainly within my range."

Hiring Manager: "Well time is about up. Do you have any questions?"

Job Seeker: "Realizing your need for someone who can do the job right, I was wondering if you had any reservations about my background?"

Hiring Manager: "Well, you don't have all the experience I was looking for, but you do seem to know how to work in this type of job."

Job Seeker: "I'm confident I would do an above average job. You wouldn't be disappointed. My other question was concerning supervision. What type of supervision will this person receive?"

Hiring Manager: "Very little actually, aside from setting quotas and weekly reports, the lister operates on his own."

Job Seeker: "That's great, I'm used to that. Those are the only questions I have at this point. The position sounds very interesting."

Hiring Manager: "Well, I have several more people to interview. You'll be hearing from us soon."

Job Seeker: "Could you tell me when I should expect to hear from you next?"

Hiring Manager: "No later than this Friday."

Job Seeker: "That's fine. Thanks for your time, I'll look forward to hearing from you."

2. In the space below, write out the strong and weak points of interview #1.

Strong Points	Weak Points

In the space below, write out the strong and weak points of interview #2.

Strong Points	Weak Points

3. Check the areas below in which you need to improve in your interview performance:
- ☐ Identify my strengths in relationship to the position.
- ☐ Develop 10 promotional statements and memorize them.
- ☐ Research the company. Get to know its products/services.
- ☐ Identify any areas of concern about my background and formulate a positive response to them.
- ☐ Find mutual points of interest with the hiring manager early in the interview.
- ☐ Ask the hiring manager about his or her needs or expectations regarding the position.
- ☐ Express enthusiasm and interest in the position if I want it.
- ☐ Focus my conversation on how I can contribute rather than what I want out of a job.
- ☐ Find out how and when I will be notified of my status in the selection process.
- ☐ Write a thank-you note as a follow-up to the interview.

4. Practice your interviewing skills with a friend.

5. Return to page 37 of Career Kit.

Sample Functional Resume

FRANK G. BRONSON
5806 24th Avenue NE
Seattle, Washington 98111
406-515-1191

OBJECTIVE: To target a career opportunity requiring strengths in:

EXPERIENCE

Implementing strategies that have impact........ Entered a "one-candidate" campaign the night before elections. Implemented a publicity blitz that included: placing signs in 150 locations, phoning 10 campus leaders to gain support, and getting on a radio show. Overnight, gained 1/3 as many votes as candidate who had campaigned for 2 weeks.

Pulling together individuals and logistics to meet needs........... As fraternity social chairman, met with campus representatives to coordinate planning of semester calendar. Scheduled and implemented 12 formal and informal events over 4-month period. Stayed within $1700 budget and surpassed attendance expectations for each event.

Coordinating and controlling projects as required............ Recruited 6 energetic and imaginative volunteers for social committee. Met weekly to brainstorm ideas and nail down details and responsibilities. Through short, productive meetings and checking back on individual assignments, kept committee productive and intact for whole semester.

Contributing ideas and perspective......... Newly formed club decided to recruit leadership through nomination ballots in mailboxes prior to a vacation period. Suggested this was poor timing and could result in loss of credibility if ballots had to be remailed. Executive committee postponed action until more advantageous time.

EDUCATION: Bachelor of Arts, Political Science
Whitman College, Walla Walla, Washington   May 1988

Diploma, The Lakeside School   1984

RELATED EXPERIENCE:

Social Committee Chairman   Tau Kappa Epsilon
Whitman College   1 Semester

Disc Jockey   KWCW Radio Station
Whitman College   1984 – Present
(Part-time)

Executive Officer for Alumni Relations   Tau Kappa Epsilon
Whitman College   1983 – 1984

Volunteer   University Hospital
Seattle, Washington

OTHER: Summer employment has included retail and temporary office work.

65

Sample Functional Resume

```
                    LAWRENCE D. MEYERS
                                              (206) 583-3859 (home)
                                              (206) 583-5836 (message)

5838 60th Avenue N.W.
Bellevue, WA   98153
                        JOB OBJECTIVE: ACCOUNTANT


QUALIFICATIONS:

Knows all phases              Four years "hands on" experience in
of general accounting...      accounts payable, accounts receivable,
                              payroll, fixed assets, and inventory.

Identifies root causes        Justified a 10% expense overrun by
for financial variances...    conducting a random audit of a 2000
                              item pricing index.

Produces reliable             Resolved a 75% error rate in financial
financial reports...          reporting by converting a 1.5 million
                              dollar accounting system from a cash
                              to accrual basis.

Masters software              Through self-teaching, modified a
programs quickly...           computer based financial model. Doubled
                              its forecasting capability and improved
                              projection accuracy by 10%.

Builds communication with     Organized and led three "in-house"
other departments...          financial workshops that equipped 100
                              managers to read and interpret financial
                              statements.

Goes the extra mile           Inherited a six month delinquent general
to get the job done...        ledger. Worked additional 60 hours
                              one month to bring books current.


WORK HISTORY:                                    Group Health Cooperative
                    Budget Analyst...........    Seattle, Washington
     1982-1983
                                                 Group Health Cooperative
                    Accountant..............     Seattle, Washington
     1980-1982
                                                 Office of Harvey C. Foys, M.D.
                    Bookkeeper..............     Seattle, Washington
     1974-1980


EDUCATION:
                    Master of Business Administration, Finance,
     August 1984    Seattle University

                    Bachelor of Arts,
     June 1973      University of Washington
```

Sample Functional Resume

```
                    SAMUEL H. FORD
                    Apartment N-202
               10003 Corning Avenue North
                  Yelm, Washington 94013
                      (216) 342-0003


OBJECTIVE:  Position as entry level claims adjustor.

                              EXPERIENCE
STRENGTHS
                         Seven years customer service experience
Satisfying customers     including service delivery, troubleshooting, and
and clients..........    advising of 100-150 customers weekly. Received
                         frequent commendations from customers for
                         personalized and prompt approach.

                         Over two years on call experience for
                         diagnosing and solving after hours equipment
Diffusing crisis/        problems with clients. Excelled at maintaining
problem situations....   client business by calmly diffusing emotion and
                         talking individual through problems and reasonable
                         solutions.

                         Reduced the error rate for all accounts by 15%
Making accurate and      in one year. Improved service calls and deliveries
fair judgement calls..   ratio by 25% over two years.

                         Achieved a personal goal of responding to all
                         off hour service inquiries within 15 minutes.
Outserving the           Taking the time to be prompt, listen and educate the
competition..........    customer saved business on occasions.

                                                          1986 - Present
EMPLOYMENT HISTORY:
                         Overall Laundry                  1983 - 1986
Account Service          Seattle, Washington
Representative
                         Abbey Medical                    1978 - 1982
Customer Service         Seattle, Washington
Representative
                         Seattle Times
Operations               Seattle, Washington
Representative
                                                          1982
                         Western Washington University
EDUCATION:                                                1980
                         Shoreline Community College
Bachelor of Arts

Associate of Arts

RELATED EXPERIENCE:
                         General knowledge of automotive repairs.
```

Sample Functional Resume

```
                    LOUISE A. ELTON
                   2015 South Urbana #F
                   Truett, Oklahoma  74095
                       (914) 480-5389
```

OBJECTIVE: A key professional position that involves improving or developing operations/administrative services.

STRENGTHS: EXPERIENCE:

Troubleshooting
* Quick response to client problems and follow up on client requests resulting in 80% repeat business with long-term clients.

* Solved information problems, organizing and summarizing it so informed decisions could be made.

Managing People and Logistics
* Managed all logistics (place, invitations, follow-up) for over 40 seminars resulting in smoothly run events and 80% attendance rate.

* Developed outline, teaching aids and/or made presentations resulting in 30% of attendees becoming clients.

Developing Systems and Information
* Developed an information system to facilitate and follow up with client phone calls and interviews.

* Developed Investment Summaries on over 30 products to streamline report completion and to better teach clients the features and benefits of product line.

Organizing to Improve Efficiency
* Systematized clients interviews and financial plan development reducing average initial consultation time from 16.5 hours to 11 hours per client.

* Coordinated work flow with associates to maximize productivity and client satisfaction.

WORK HISTORY:

Financial Planner   Southwest Planning Group   1986
                     Tulsa, Oklahoma

Financial Planner   ComPlan Financial Services, Inc.   1982 - 1985
                     Tulsa, Oklahoma

EDUCATION:

Master of Business Administration, Finance   1984
University of Tulsa

Bachelor of Arts   1981
Oral Roberts University

Sample Functional Resume

```
                    SUSAN JANE OSBORN
                304 West Comestock Street
                Seattle, Washington  98119
                       (201) 242-7401

OBJECTIVE:  To offer quality service to groups and/or individuals via the
            hospitality/travel industry.

                                    EXPERIENCE
STRENGTHS
                            As event coordinator, assisted ten clients in
Identify client needs       determining setup, food service, timelines for
and objectives.......       delivery, staffing needs and professional services.
                            Most frequent comment received was "thank you for
                            your efforts, we could relax and enjoy the event..."

                            Assigned task of computerizing 8000 client records.
                            Over six months, identified best method to organize
Coordinating projects       records, selected software, entered all data, and
from idea to finished       trained staff on reading printouts.  Efforts cut
product..............       staff time and expense by 30%.

                            Coordinated a four hour open house for 100 guests
                            including creating invitations, food preparation,
Minimizing cost/expense     serving and cleanup.  Quality of event resulted in
without compromising        several referrals.  Through wise shopping and
quality..............       creative use of resources the project was completed
                            for $100.

                            In two retail positions, was asked to create displays
                            to feature new products, styles, or fabrics.  In both
Knowing what is             instances, ended up designing and forming many
visually/aesthetically      future displays.
appropriate..........
                            Produced gifts and crafts for sale during two
Tracking resources,         holiday seasons.  Closely tracking all materials,
costs, and timelines        time, and production costs resulted in a fourfold
for future use and          increase in production and noticeable increase in
improvement..........       profits.
                                                              1986 - Present
WORK HISTORY:
                            Talbots                           1984 - 1986
     Sales Associate        Seattle, Washington

                            Burden Bearers Inc.               1980 - 1985
     Receptionist/          Seattle, Washington
     Special Events
                            Nancy's Sewing Basket             1982 - Present
     Sales Clerk/Consultant Seattle, Washington

                            Susan Osborn
     Custom Clothing        Custom Sewing
     Specialist             Seattle, Washington
```

Sample Chronological Resume

Sample Chronological Resume

Sample Chronological Resume

CLAY DUNCAN (306) 775-2300

13566 23rd Avenue West, #1
Snohomish, Washington 98145

OBJECTIVE: Seeking a warehouse position requiring strengths in shipping and receiving, purchasing, and organization.

EMPLOYMENT HISTORY:

Warehouseman World Concern, Seattle, Washington 1984 - Present

Prepared and packaged seed and medical supplies to be shipped to 20 foreign countries. Utilized crates, sea containers, drums, and boxes.

ACCOMPLISHMENTS

* Packed over 40, 1280 cubic foot, sea containers within a 3-day preparation time. Met all shipping deadlines and received no returned damaged freight.

* Recruited and trained 45 volunteer staff to expedite shipping on 4 large projects. Met all deadlines.

* Purchased all warehouse packing supplies on a bi-monthly and semi-annual basis. Saved $1,000 on boxes through shopping around for best buys. Kept within budget.

Warehouse Manager/Assistant Pride and Suther Inc., Seattle, Washington 1978 - 1984

Managed shipping and receiving of plumbing and heating supplies to 40 plumbers and fitters. Shipped 80% of materials to Alaska via bargelines, trucking, air freight and express mail. Tracked all orders, materials and supplies.

ACCOMPLISHMENTS

* Contacted 5 packaging manufacturers to check out pricing. Found best deal and bulk ordered supplies. Saved company $500 in annual costs.

* Coordinating bidding with major suppliers on 8 projects valued at 25 million dollars. Efforts reduced costs 6 - 8%.

* Processed and shipped thousands of orders over 6-year period. Less than 10 shipments ever returned damaged. Quality of work resulted in promotion to manager.

EDUCATION: General Education Diploma 1978

Sample Chronological Resume

```
                    DAVID B. HUMES
                    162 Southwest Place
                    Granton, Texas 72615


                    Finance Administration
OBJECTIVE:

EMPLOYMENT HISTORY:  Corporate Controller, Foster's International
                     Accounting
1981 - 1984          Dallas, Texas

                     Responsible for all financial and accounting
                     activity for company of 2200 employees, managed
                     a staff of 125 employees.

                     Achieved a team approach with both the management
                     and operations departments. With user input
                     from all areas, revised over 200 computer
                     formats and decreased errors in budgeting and
                     financial reports by 10%.

                     Assistant Controller, Hyatt House West
                     Incline Village, Arizona

1977 - 1981          Responsible for daily operation of data
                     processing, revenue audits, and financial
                     statements, managed 75 professional staff.

                     Turned around an inefficient, unreliable
                     financial reporting system in two years. Cut
                     costs by 15% while improving accuracy of
                     reports and audits by 20%.

                     Staff Accountant, James and Associates
                     San Diego, California

1976 - 1977          Performed over 300 extensive audits. Re-
                     organized audit procedures to eliminate
                     duplication of effort in final reporting.
                     Suggestions saved firm $1,000 in needless
                     overhead expense per audit.

EDUCATION:           B.S. in Accounting, San Diego State, California
```

Sample Cover letter

Sample Cover letter

Sample Cover letter

November 26, 1984

Jeff D. Christensen
Business Manager
Snoqualmie Valley School District #410
P.O. Box 400
Snoqualmie, WA 98065

Dear Mr. Christensen,

Thank you for clarifying the qualifications for the Food Service Supervisor position. As I have familiarized myself with school food service, I see a natural tie between my experience and the responsibilities of this position.

In serving over 300,000 meals to students of all ages, I understand what it takes to provide meals that meet nutritional guidelines yet maintain broad student appeal.

Seven years experience with non-profit organizations has given me a solid knowledge of government commodities and reimbursement food service programs. Having worked in all phases of food service, supervised a staff of 16, and maintained positive work relationships with both program and administrative staff, I understand the "support function" of food service.

Knowing how to operate on a tight budget without cutting quality has always been a strength of mine. Through wise buying and scheduling, I have cut purchasing costs up to 20% and labor costs by 10% in each of my previous positions.

If you need a Food Service Supervisor who is student-oriented, knowledgeable about government programs, skilled at developing cooperative work relationships, and able to minimize expenses without sacrificing quality, I would welcome the opportunity to talk more specifically with you.

Enclosed are my application and resume for your review.

Sincerely,

Don D. Alexander

Enclosure

Sample Cover letter

January 5, 1985

Mr. Jerry Smith
Delmore, Smith and Mcgee, Inc.
1984 1st West Suite 508
Seattle, WA 98124

Dear Mr. Smith,

When a heavy workload requires you to seek additional help in architectural illustration, you want someone who can meet deadlines without cutting quality. You need a specialist, someone who understands architecture but excels in graphic presentation.

An architect by training, I have specialized in illustration for 16 years. My range of experience extends from residential to commercial, and includes both black and white and full-color illustration. As a free-lance illustrator, I have served over 40 clients on 200 separate projects. The high quality of my work has always resulted in repeat business.

A person who enjoys variety and change, I am seeking to expand my services to a wider clientele. The enclosed brochure will give you a sample of what I can contribute to your firm.

I would appreciate the opportunity to meet briefly with you to discuss how I might be of present or future service. I will telephone you in the near future to further pursue this possibility.

Sincerely yours,

Larry F. Johnson

Enclosure

Sample Thank you note for Job Interview

June 6, 1985

Mr. John Clark
Advance Ministries
1584 McGraw Street
Columbus, OH 58375

Dear Mr. Clark,

Just a brief note to thank you for taking the time to talk with me about the Media Manager position at Advance Ministries.

Your interest in expanding contact with radio stations across the country was particularly exciting. As I mentioned, the promotion concepts I implemented in my current position boosted our radio participation by 30%.

Under your direction, I am confident we could enlarge the scope of Advance Ministries through radio. What a challenge to be involved in a dynamic, growing ministry! I will look forward to hearing from you. Thanks again for an informative and professional interview.

Sincerely,

Edwin L. Hamilton

Sample Thank you note for Job Interview

February 19, 1984

Mr. Randy Tiede
Stimpson and Associates
1845 5th Avenue North
Lynnwood, WA 98115

Dear Mr. Tiede,

Do you always conduct such stimulating job interviews? Your questions and our discussion about the accounting position were both interesting and exciting!

Finding a job that demands the unique blend of qualifications and experience I possess is a challenge. As both you and Mr. Graham stated, my background is well suited for the job.

Under your leadership, I am sure my experience in converting and troubleshooting accounting systems would be an asset to the department as you embark upon a major systems conversion. The other responsibilities you outlined were equally interesting.

Thanks again for a professional but personable interview. I am confident that working together we could develop the accounting department to enhance its effectiveness and efficiency.

To that end, I will look forward to further discussion of your needs and expectations for this position.

Sincerely,

Joanne W. Keihl

Sample Thank you note for Job Interview

April 13, 1985

Donna J. Fulkerson
Southshore Community Hospital
1583 Norway Drive South
Lacy, WA 98583

Dear Ms. Fulkerson,

Thank you for taking the time to discuss the Administrative Assistant opening in your department.

In reflecting on our conversation, I am confident that I could provide the type of professional, independent, and fast-paced performance that you need. Being flexible but well organized has always been my strong suit.

Your candor about my "limited experience" was refreshing. Let me assure you that inexperience has never hindered me from exceeding performance expectations. My references will confirm this.

The plans and direction you outlined in our interview were intriguing. I would welcome the opportunity to contribute to their accomplishment. To that end, I will look forward to hearing from you.

Thanks again for your courtesy and interest.

Sincerely,

Diana R. Sattler

Diana R. Sattler

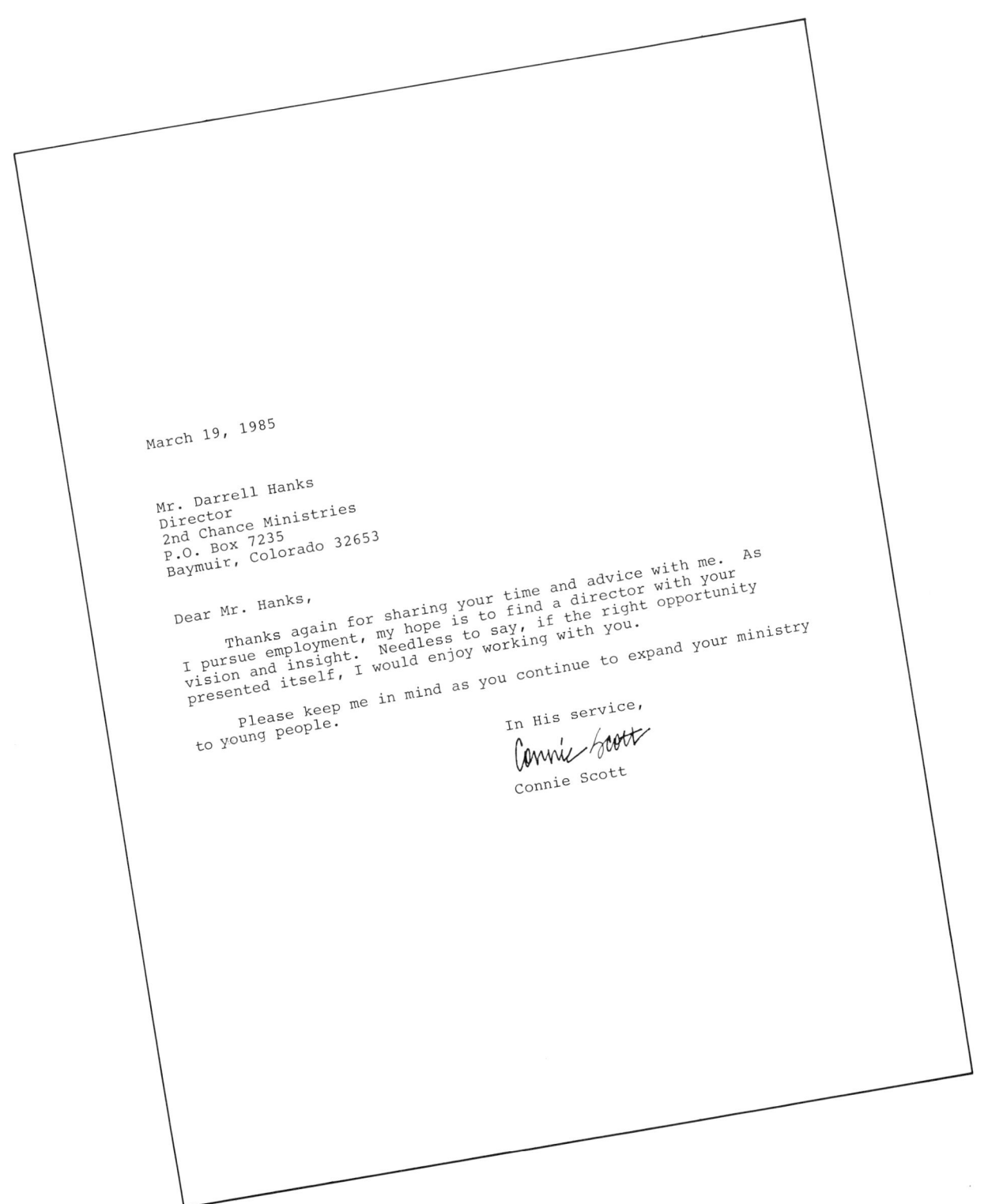

Sample Thank you note for Referral Interview

March 19, 1985

Mr. Darrell Hanks
Director
2nd Chance Ministries
P.O. Box 7235
Baymuir, Colorado 32653

Dear Mr. Hanks,

Thanks again for sharing your time and advice with me. As I pursue employment, my hope is to find a director with your vision and insight. Needless to say, if the right opportunity presented itself, I would enjoy working with you.

Please keep me in mind as you continue to expand your ministry to young people.

In His service,

Connie Scott

Connie Scott

Sample Thank you note for Referral Interview

May 15, 1984

Ms. Joan Crawford
Activities Coordinator
City Conventions
3527 West Main Street
Detroit, Michigan 49203

Dear Ms. Crawford,

As I am sure you are aware, when re-directing one's career, the search process can at times seem overwhelming.

However, meeting people like you along the way makes all the difference. Your advice and suggestions last Thursday were extremely helpful.

In addition to a much needed "shot in the arm" you gave me an excellent lead. I am meeting with Roger Capron this Thursday. As we discussed, I will follow up with you in two weeks for an update.

Thanks again for your time, support, and direction.

Sincerely,

Bill Stohler

Sample Thank you note for Referral Interview

July 15, 1984

Mr. Paul Halter
Invesco Services
P.O. Box 39
Tacoma, WA 98485

Dear Paul,

I thoroughly enjoyed our meeting last week and the opportunity to discuss various ways to market financial services. Your grasp of the industry and its problems shows why it is necessary at times to have the perspective of a consultant.

I appreciated your suggestions of companies that may have an interest in me, and your offer to initially contact the Presidents on my behalf. With your approval, I will wait one week and then contact each gentleman directly.

Again, thank you for your assistance. I'll let you know how the meetings go.

Sincerely,

Mike C. Jones

Mike C. Jones